"In his delightfully written book of commentary on commentaries, Norman Cohen shares with his readers what, for many years, he has been giving his students: rare erudition, sensitivity, and insight."
—**Elie Wiesel**

"A delightful and instructive book."
—**Library Journal**

How do I find greater wholeness in my life and in my family's life?

The stress of late-20th-century living only brings new variations to timeless personal struggles. The people described by the biblical writers of Genesis were in situations and relationships very much like our own, and their stories still speak to us because they are about the same basic problems *we* deal with every day.

Learning from **Adam and Eve,** can we find the courage not only to face our other side, but to draw strength from it? Learning from **Leah and Rachel,** can we stop competing with our loved ones, and begin to accept them and find ourselves? **Sarah, Hagar, Lot, Ishmael and Isaac, Rebekkah, Joseph and his brothers, Jacob and Esau**…this vibrant cast of characters offers us new ways of understanding ourselves and our families and healing our lives.

In this intriguing retelling of conflict between husband and wife, father and son, brothers, and sisters, a modern master of biblical interpretation brings us greater understanding of the ancient biblical text—and of ourselves.

Self, Struggle & Change

Family Conflict Stories in Genesis
and
Their Healing Insights
for Our Lives

Norman J. Cohen

Jewish Lights Publishing

Self, Struggle & Change:
Family Conflict Stories in Genesis and
Their Healing Insights for Our Lives

©1995 by Norman J. Cohen

Cover: Tree Image, Image Copyright ©1996 PhotoDisc, Inc.

Library of Congress Cataloging-in-Publication Data

Cohen, Norman J.
Self, struggle & change: family conflict stories in Genesis and their healing insights for our lives / Norman J. Cohen.
p.   cm.
Includes bibliographical references.
ISBN-13: 978-1-879045-66-8
ISBN-10: 1-879045-66-4
1. Family—Biblical teaching. 2. Bible. O.T. Genesis—Meditations. I. Title II. Title: Self, struggle, and change.
BS1238.F34C64 1995
94-39880   222'.110922—dc20   CIP

ISBN: 978-1-68336-287-6 (hc)

Manufactured in the United States of America
Cover design: Lindy Gifford

Published by JEWISH LIGHTS Publishing
www.jewishlights.com

To the memory of my grandfather,

R. Hayyim Baruch,

whom we affectionately called Shorty.

*He instilled in me his love of Judaism
and the Jewish people, and his
passion for Torah*

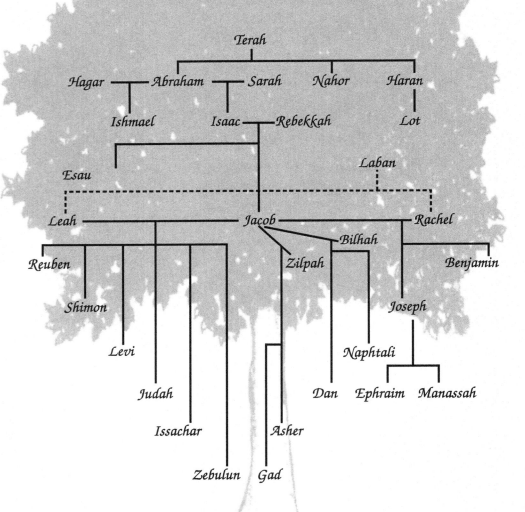

Contents

Acknowledgments   9

Introduction   11

CHAPTER ONE: ADAM AND EVE
The Different Sides of Each of Us   17

CHAPTER TWO: CAIN AND ABEL
The Conflict between Good and Evil   35

CHAPTER THREE: ISHMAEL AND ISAAC
The Tensions between Siblings   63

CHAPTER FOUR: JACOB AND ESAU
Twins Struggle for Identity   95

CHAPTER FIVE: LEAH AND RACHEL
Seeking My Sister; Finding Myself   125

CHAPTER SIX: JOSEPH AND HIS BROTHERS
The Two Sides Meet Again   149

EPILOGUE: THE TWO MESSIAHS
When the Different Sides Come Together   189

Endnotes   197

Suggested Further Readings   209

About Jewish Lights Publishing   222

Acknowledgments

This book is a product of my own spiritual journey which began as a young teenager sitting next to my paternal grandfather in the synagogue on Shabbat afternoon. Watching his face radiate from the power of the words of Torah as he and his friends studied together, I wanted to feel as he did. I, too, wanted to be transformed by the biblical narratives and carried away by them.

So when I studied at the Hebrew Union College-Jewish Institute of Religion and then began teaching at the New York School, I came to realize that the object of studying and analyzing the text was not merely to understand how and when it came to be and what it meant for those who shaped it, but also what it can mean for us in our own lives. It is in this light that I owe the greatest debt of thanks to the students with whom I have studied over the past twenty years. They have demanded that the Torah speak to us directly, addressing our questions and concerns.

However, my personal journey has been shaped most by my family, without whom I could not have reached this point in my life. They have taught me that immersion into the Torah text must shape who we are as human beings and our priorities in life. My parents, Irving and Molly Cohen z"l, my brother Marvin, our children, Leora, Abby, Noah, Mali and Ilan, and my wife Terry, have blessed me with their unconditional love and concern. The journey has not always been easy. Creating a blended family of seven could only happen because of five terrific and flexible young children, and a wife who is a constant support and partner. I am indebted to Terry for making our life and home as wonderful as they are.

I also owe a great deal to many colleagues and friends at the College-Institute in New York and in the Jewish community, several of whom have read parts of this manuscript. Though they will go unnamed, they should know how much their support, advice and concern have buoyed me and have made the many hours I spend at H.U.C.-J.I.R. so rewarding and full. I also want to thank Dr. Alfred Gottschalk, President of the College-Institute, for giving me the opportunity to be part of our wonderful seminary and for his continuing support, and Dr. Eugene Mihaly, my mentor at our Cincinnati campus, who taught me to hear the music of the text.

I also owe much to Marie Cantlon, who edited the book. Her patient guidance, insightful questions and vision helped me find the words and the voice through which to speak. In addition, Sandra Korinchak of Jewish Lights invested an extraordinary amount of time and energy in polishing the manuscript. However, without the friendship, urging, wise counsel and trust of Stuart Matlins, founder of Jewish Lights Publishing, this book would not have been possible. Working with him has been a true labor of love.

In sharing this book with you, I share my life and my own struggles. More importantly, however, I share my passion for the study of Torah in the hope that you will come to see the text as a source of life-giving water. "Let all who are thirsty come and drink" (Isaiah 55:1).

N.J.C.
On Martha's Vineyard
July 25, 1994
17 Av, 5754

Introduction

The contemporary writer Sam Shepard said that somewhere there is a myth about the wolf and the lamb, and that human beings carry both inside. The process of keeping alive is trying to carry on a balance between these two parts, because one is always trying to devour the other.[1]

Shepard's portrayal of the conflict between our different sides is typical of much artistic expression. In his writing we frequently see the roles that pairs of brothers play. These characters clearly represent the struggle within the writer himself, and in each and every one of us. Each brother represents distinctions between male/female, divine/human, good/evil, and life/death, which are always followed by attempts to bridge them.[2]

Even though the intelligent modern reader or viewer has no problem identifying tensions between opposites within each human being as represented by pairs of literary characters or mythic heroes, such as Romulus and Remus, to whom the founding of Rome is attributed, the same readers often fail to discern these powerfully relevant patterns in religious texts such as the Bible. This is because most of us do not take the Bible seriously. We see it as an antiquated remnant of the Ancient Near East or we view the study of and reflection upon the biblical text as a religious school exercise, relegated to the education of children. We who never have the opportunity to grapple actively with our sacred stories have a difficult time appreciating how they can speak directly to us and to our life situations. We do not see how they possibly can help us understand ourselves as spouses, parents, children, lovers, and friends, or shape the direction of our lives.

Yet, the power and relevance of the Bible is demonstrated by its enduring presence throughout all parts of western culture. By confronting the biblical text, whether we see it as divinely given or the product of divinely inspired human beings, and immersing ourselves in these sacred stories, we can gain a better sense of the meaning of our own baffling dramas. This, in turn, can affect the nature of our lives and our priorities.[3]

To appreciate the importance of the Bible and gain insight about ourselves from it, both Jews and Christians can use the process of midrash: The attempt to find contemporary meaning in the biblical text. The term midrash comes from the Hebrew root *darash* which means to seek, search or demand (meaning from the biblical text). The starting point of our search for personal meaning is the Bible itself. This is the first level of our midrashic interpretation. By using all the possible knowledge of the Bible at our disposal—philological, literary, historical, archeological, sociological, theological—we can approximate what the biblical writers meant in any given narrative. Our task at the outset is to imbibe the power and flavor of the biblical text itself, attending closely to every word, every detail. Each generation, each reader, can approach the text anew and draw meaning from it. By filtering our sacred stories through the prism of nearly two millennia of rabbinic interpreters, Jews and non-Jews alike can learn from their sense of the text's meaning. It is vital to remember that the great rabbinic sages were human beings too. And as they responded to the text, they responded to the pressures of their own life situations. They had no choice but to read the text through the lens of the political, religious, and socio-cultural conditions under which they lived. Their interpretations embody their polemical replies to the challenges to Jewish survival which they faced living under the Greeks, Romans, Persians,

Babylonians, Christians and Moslems. Yet, at the very same time, they also responded to universal questions of meaning raised by every generation and by all people: What does it mean to be a human being created in God's image? How can we make our personal lives better? Can we perfect our world? Their questions are our questions and their interpretations reach across time and space to touch and teach us. This then is the second level of our midrashic study: To open ourselves to the myriad rabbinic interpretations of the biblical narratives.

However, it is not enough for us to read the interpretations found in the classic midrashim and in the Talmud. Reading a sacred text forces self-involvement and self-reflection, and it is through our own entry into the text that meaning surfaces. Thus with every story we study, we learn not only about what we are reading, but also about ourselves. In deciphering a text, we bring to the fore elements of our own being of which we may not always be conscious. We respond to our own questions and dilemmas.

This then is the final stage of the midrashic process.[4] To gain insight from the biblical text, it is incumbent upon each of us to read the text slowly. Our task is to pay attention to every word, phrase, metaphor, and symbol. And since the biblical narratives are so terse and the sketches of biblical characters so fragmentary, the inclusion or even the exclusion of any particular word or phrase may be of great significance. Choices of syntax, narrative structures, the repetition of motifs, as well as selective silences can all be seen as crucial threads in weaving a fabric of meaning. Generally the biblical writers present only that which the reader absolutely needs in order to understand the flow and the thrust of story. This challenges the reader to fill in the gaps, supplying what is meant but is at times not stated. The obliqueness of the biblical material is that which beckons readers from every generation and every faith to enter the text, to delight in discovering the depth of its meaning, and to enrich their own lives.[5]

It is the sketchiness of detail that invariably draws us especially to the personalities of the Book of Genesis. We are confronted by vaguely drawn descriptions of characters who, generation after generation, struggle with themselves and especially with their siblings. Genesis presents the reader with stories of family rivalry which embody the basic tension between contrasting personalities with whom we can identify almost immediately.

Such conflicts between different personalities are probably adapted from common patterns found in folklore, such as the dispute between the shepherd and the farmer, or the conflict between brothers.[6] Yet, the very forces in conflict always seem to be parts of a whole, of one and the same being, with a constant shift between moments of contrast and moments of similarity.[7] However, the people of the Ancient Near East perceived the struggle to be only among the external forces of nature, never suspecting that they were really seeing the paradoxical nature of their own personalities.

Modern psychology has taught us that each human being has a complex personality made up of a variety of positive and negative traits. We tend to repress the negative tendencies which constantly function as part of our unconscious.[8] For some of us, these parts of our personalities have gained a stronghold and dominate our lives, though we may be unaware of them. For all of us, channeling these tendencies toward constructive ends is not possible until we can recognize them, admitting to ourselves that these forces are real and present within us. This is the first step in the process of individual growth; in our integrating the disparate elements—the good and evil, the divine and human—into a better functioning whole.

The Genesis narratives in particular can serve as vehicles

of insight into our own personalities as well as the dynamic tensions within our own families. They can help us see ourselves as brothers and sisters, and as parents and children. This is because the biblical writers attempt to express through their stories what we are as human beings, with all our conflicting qualities—greed, generosity, lust, love, fear, courage, selfishness, compassion and much more.[9] Since it is through a wrestling with the sacred stories of Torah and with the complex personages delineated in them that we can begin to take an honest look at ourselves, it is precisely upon our own reading of the biblical text that our search for wholeness and holiness is contingent.

Our recreating the text, the creation of our own modern midrash, must be moored in the traditions of the past. I have cited in the sidebars all the sources which I have used, both the core biblical passages as well as the midrashic texts, so that the reader can better understand the basis upon which the interpretation is built. Yet, the creation of midrash is an open task for each new reader. It is never considered complete. For whenever a passionate reader grants any text an appropriate reading, an interpretation or expansion which helps him or her as a human being, and fosters growth, the Torah will come alive. At that instant it will be working in the life of that very reader.[10]

The starting point in the process of creating our own modern midrash, as already intimated, is paying close attention to the Torah text itself. Our task is to open the stories of sibling rivalry and family conflict in the Book of Genesis in such a way that they speak directly to us. Therefore, we must begin "in the beginning."

By imbibing the power of the words of *Bereshit* (Genesis), from the creation of humankind as male and female in the Garden of Eden through their struggles with themselves, their siblings and with God, culminating with Jacob's blessings of his twelve sons, we may come to a better understanding of our own true natures. As we confront these sacred stories, we not only learn about them, but they can teach us about who we are and what we can become. We who have been driven from the Garden can find a path back to our original wholeness. The text is a mirror that reflects a picture of each reader who has the courage to peer into it with an open mind and a willing heart that reaches toward heaven.

CHAPTER ONE

ADAM AND EVE

The Different Sides of Each of Us

We, like our primordial ancestor Adam, are made up of many sides. We, too, struggle to live with the tension between our God-like potential and our very human natures. Like the first human being, we also were created with both male and female traits, though we rarely are in touch with that other aspect of our being.

Adam was driven from the Garden of Eden, separated from the Divine presence, just as the male and female were separated in the Creation story. They were relegated to survive in the world outside of paradise in order to bond together into an even more meaningful unity. True wholeness can only come through our personal struggle to overcome the disparate elements in us. And only then, after coming in touch with our fragmentation, isolation and loneliness, can we reach the Garden of our maturity.

Like Adam and Eve, we wonder how long it will take to return to our original wholeness. We wonder if we have the strength and the courage to confront our other side, struggle with it, and thereby find our true selves in the process?

Just imagine what Adam might say after reading the first two chapters of Genesis that describe the Creation. "Can you believe this story? It doesn't give any information about how God formed me and what I was like. Many of the important details are left out. The reader hasn't the slightest idea of what happened on the Sixth Day or what I went through."

Adam is right. From the very beginning of the Book of Genesis, we are struck by the terseness of the biblical narrative. The text tends to raise more questions than it answers. Even at the culmination of the Six Days of Creation, we are given only several descriptive fragments, and these seem to be problematic and at times contradictory. We are left with tantalizing questions, such as exactly how Adam and Eve were created and what their basic natures were.

Yet, by paying attention to the information given us, by focusing on the possible meanings and symbolism of every word—by reading the text midrashically—we can gain deep insight from the fragmentary description. Listen to the words of the text and imbibe their power.

The Tension between Divine and Human: Struggling with Our Two Sides

"Let us make the...
Genesis 1:26–27.

At the end of the Sixth Day of Creation after the appearance of all the animals, God's voice rings forth from the heavens one final time, saying: "*Let us* make the human being in *our* image, after *our* likeness. And they shall have dominion over the fish of the sea, the birds of the sky....And God created Adam in the Divine's image, in the image of God did the Divine create him; male and female God created them."

The description of Adam's creation opens in a rather peculiar manner. Why does God speak in the first person plural? To whom is God talking? Most Jewish commentators understand this to be either the biblical writer's use of the

[18]

majestic plural or an allusion to God's retinue of angels.

In the Midrash, God frequently is pictured as conversing with the angels, especially regarding the creation of humankind. Using our imaginations, we can envision the ministering angels arguing about the merit of Adam's creation. One group pressed God to create this first human being, while the second tried to convince God not to proceed. The angels of Love and Righteousness felt God should create humankind because men and women in the future will perform acts of love and righteousness; the angels of Truth and Justice argued against the creation since human beings will be full of falsehood and strife. In the end, God ignored the pleas of the second group of angels and went about creating Adam.

we can envision... Bereshit Rabbah 8:5.

If we understand such midrashim figuratively, as I think they are intended, then the angels represent different aspects of the Godhead itself, different attributes of the Divine. This notion is consistent with the manner in which God is generally presented in the Midrash. For example, God is said to possess both the attributes of Mercy and Justice, *Middat ha-Din* and *Middat ha-Rachamim.*

attributes of Mercy... See B.T. *Berahot* 7a, Vayiqra Rabbah 29:6 and Midrash Psalms 56:10.

It is clear, then, that our text in Genesis ("Let us make the human being in our image, after our likeness") speaks of the one God's many sides. God possesses different characteristics, even though God is an absolute unity. God's different, even seemingly contradictory attributes are part of a perfect whole.

We should note, however, that all these midrashim also underscore the contradictory sides of the human being as well. We, like the Divine in whose image we are created, are capable of acts of love and kindness, but at the same time we can be dishonest and hurtful to others. We, too, possess different sides.

Most interestingly, our very same Genesis text seems also to emphasize the complex nature of the human being. This is evident from the obvious interchange and shift between singular and plural subjects and objects—listen to the text again: "And God said: Let us make *the human being* in our image....And *they* shall have dominion over the fish....And God created *Adam* in the Divine's image, in the image of God the Divine created *him*, male and female God created *them*. And God blessed *them* and said to *them*, "Be fruitful and multiply and replenish the earth."

"And God said:...
Genesis 1:26-28.

A similar shift between the singular creation called "Adam" and the allusion to his divided nature is found in a parallel description of the creation of the first human being a bit later in the text: "This is the record of Adam's line. When God created Adam, God made him in the likeness of the Divine; male and female God created them. And when they were created, God blessed them and called them Adam (or man)."

"This is the record...
Genesis 5:1-2.

The human being, who appears at the end of the Sixth Day, after all the animals, is created in the Divine likeness. Adam indeed is unlike all of God's other creations. He is God-like.

Yet, there is another sharply contrasting description of the creation of humankind in Genesis. In this second Creation story we are told that "The Lord formed *(va-yyitzer)* the human being from the dust of the earth. [God] blew into his nostrils the breath of life and the man became a living being."[1]

"The Lord formed...
Genesis 2:7.

It is striking that the verb utilized here is *yatzar* which generally refers to human artisanship. God is pictured as a craftsperson who erects a building or a potter who shapes a pot on a wheel. The choice of verbs is fitting, since in this version of the Creation story the biblical writer stresses that Adam was created not in the image of God, but rather from the inanimate clay of the earth. He was created from the *adamah* (the earth), which would soon be cursed, and he, *Adam*, in his finiteness, bears the essential quality of the

which would soon be cursed...
Genesis 3:17.

earthly realm. Though God indeed "blew into [Adam's] nostrils the breath of life and he became a living being," he was not destined to be immortal. Each of us, too, is born, and has the ability to propagate, but we, like our primordial ancestor, will eventually die. We will return to the earth.

The very different emphases in the two Creation stories underscore for us the fact that we human beings possess an earthly dimension as well as a God-like quality. Though we are finite, we are suffused with the breath of life, the spirit of the Divine. Built into us is the tension between the physical and the spiritual, a tension expressed in a well-known hasidic saying: Each person should keep two slips of paper in his or her pocket. One should read: "For my sake the world was created," while the other states: "I am but dust and ashes."

A saying of R. Simha Bunam of Pzhysha.

This polarity is highlighted by the rabbis in a number of classic texts. One such midrash is built upon the rabbis' sensitivity to the fact that the verb used in our passage in Genesis 2:7, *va-yyitzer* (and [God] formed), is really quite odd. We rarely ever find it spelled with a double "y" (*yod*).[2] Therefore our sages stress that the two *yods* indicate there were two distinct aspects in the creation of the primordial human being. In the course of discussing the nature of the two conflicting sides, the rabbis highlight Adam's earthly as well as God-like nature, his good and evil instincts. You see, they say, God created human beings with four attributes the angels possess and four which animals possess. The earthly qualities are that we eat, drink, procreate and then die. In contrast, our celestial attributes are that we, like the ministering angels, stand upright, speak, understand and see. Rabbi Tifdai suggests that, like the angels, human beings were created in the image of God, and, like the animals, can procreate. According to R. Tifdai, God reasoned that if Adam were created only like the celestial beings, he would live forever, and if Adam were created like the ani-

[21]

mals, he would die and not live in the future. Therefore, God decided to create Adam of both the celestial and terrestial elements. The result is that although human beings are imperfect, even frail, and must surely die, we each have the potential for immortality.

We, like our primordial ancestor Adam, struggle to live with the tension between our God-like potential and our very human natures. We even wonder ourselves how at one moment we can perform acts of love and kindness that represent our highest potential, yet immediately thereafter can be hurtful, even to those whom we profess to love. In our most honest self-reflections, we know what we are capable of doing—both the good and the bad.

There is no more striking example of the polarity within which human beings live than Oskar Schindler, the German entrepreneur who saved some 1,100 Polish Jewish lives during the Holocaust. Schindler was a drunkard and womanizer of the first order, who mistreated his wife while maintaining relationships with several girlfriends. Businessman that he was, during the German war effort, he realized that he could produce kitchenware and sell it on the black market and make huge profits.

Yet, in the course of building his enamelware business, he got to know the 1,100 Polish Jews who worked for him and came to treat them as human beings. Unlike his Nazi colleagues, he could not countenance any effort to dehumanize his Jews. Schindler built his own barracks so they would not have to be put in a concentration camp, and he prevented their deportation by bribing German officers and forging documents. All this at the risk of his own life. In the end he was even willing to move his entire factory to the Sudetenland in late 1944 to save his Jews.

Perhaps what best symbolized the two sides of Oskar Schindler was the ring presented to him on V.E. Day, May 8, 1945, when he fled as Allied forces approached. Gold teeth taken from one of the workers were fashioned into a ring inscribed to Schindler and given to him by those whose lives he had saved. That ring epitomized their respect for this human being who literally gave them their lives. Sixteen years later, Oskar Schindler came to Israel and was welcomed by a throng of those he protected. They asked him about the ring, and he replied that he had sold it to buy schnapps![3] We are all like Oskar Schindler. We, who can be kind, generous and good to others, struggle at times with the other side of ourselves. We, too, who are created a little lower than the angels, sometimes are nothing more than tarnished angels.

God Created Adam Both Male and Female: Becoming a Unity of Opposites

The Creation story not only emphasizes that the first human being, Adam, was a combination of the Divine and the human, but also that at one and the same time he was male and female. Both his male and female sides were clearly rooted in God's own nature, since we read, "When God created Adam, [God] made him in the likeness of God; male and female [God] created them. And when they were created, [God] blessed them and called them Adam." The primordial human being was created as a unity of opposites.

"When God created... Genesis 5:1-2.

In various midrashic texts, the shifts between singular and plural in this as well as other verses are understood to mean that in creating Adam *ha-Rishon*, the first human being, God created a hermaphrodite, male and female in one physical entity.

In one such text, Rabbi Jeremiah b. Leazer (4th century) argued that when the Holy One created Adam, God created him as an *androgynos*. (Normally, the term *androgynos* is taken to refer to a person with both male and female genitalia.) Rabbi Jeremiah goes on to explain that

In one such text... Bereshit Rabbah 8:1. See also Vayiqra Rabbah 14:1, and Midrash Psalms 139:5.

[23]

Adam was made up of two different bodies joined together. In a similar manner, Rabbi Samuel b. Nahman (4th century) believed God created Adam double-faced, connected back to back, then split Adam and made two separate human beings. Traditions such as these clearly imply that in creating the first human being, God created a person with two distinct sides that had to be separated. The original unity was cleaved in two, thereby creating the man and the woman.

With a bit of imagination, we can picture the unity called Adam, made up of two distinct sides back to back, which could never see each other. What must it have been like for each half of the primordial human being to feel whole, but always be aware that there was another side shadowing it from behind, and never knowing exactly what that other half was like? The irony, of course, is that the only way for the two sides of Adam to come to know each other was for this first human creation to be split in two. Though created together, Adam's male and female sides could never be unified if they were to remain turned away from each other. Only by standing over against and facing each other could they ever come to know one another and become truly one. The reunification of the two sides, the male and female in Adam, would be far better than their original unity, for it would be based upon each other's knowledge and acceptance of the other.

Are we so unlike that first human being in the Garden of Eden who slowly became aware that there was another side to him/her which was ever-present but hidden from view? Many of us, especially we who are male, may be oblivious to that other side, though we desperately must come to know it if we are ever to grow into our whole selves. We males must come in touch with the softness and responsiveness that may be hidden deeply in us and, in so doing, allow it to become more manifest in all our actions, especially in the way we interact with others.

For example, people frequently ask if there is a difference between male and female clergy, specifically relating to their style of leadership within the congregational setting. Perhaps the difference between Moses' and Miriam's songs sung at the crossing of the Red Sea can be instructive here. The narrative tells us, "Then Moses and Israel sang this song to God." However, there is a question regarding who did the singing at the Sea, since the verb in Hebrew, *yashir*, is singular, and could mean that only Moses sang and the people merely listened to his words.[4]

The narrative tells us...
Exodus 15:1.

In the tradition it is generally understood that Moses did most of the singing, and at best Israel followed his lead by echoing or imitating his words and melody. Moses is the model of the strong male leader who has a clear sense of what God wants of us and teaches his words or melody to his constituents. To be sure, it is important for laypeople to experience the vision and the song of the Jewish people as transmitted by their leaders. Every Jew who aspires to leadership must have a sense of what he or she believes and what it means to be a Jew, a member of a covenanted people.

In the tradition...
The Mekhilta d'Rabbi Ishmael, *Massekhta d'Shirta,* *parashah* 1.

Yet there is another model of leadership present at the Sea, which usually goes unnoticed because it seems less significant. Though Miriam's song is only one line (v. 21) as compared to the nineteen-verse song of Moses (vv. 1–19), it is poignantly different. Whereas Moses' singing is described by the verb *yashir,* he sang his song to the people, we learn that Miriam actually responded to her sisters. (The Hebrew describes Miriam's singing as *"ve-ta'an lahem Miriam,* Miriam responded to them. The verb used is *ta'an,* which comes from the root *anah.*) In effect, Moses sang in front of the congregation; Miriam in contrast was able to draw out the song of others. She empowered them to sing their own songs.

The challenge, of course, is for each of us who are blessed

to play a religious leadership role to come in touch with that other side of ourselves and make it a more active part of us. If we are male, then we must search for the softer, more open and responsive parts of our being, so as to help us respond better to others. This will enable us to teach others that they, too, can sing God's song. And if we are female, we can begin to draw on the more aggressive sides of ourselves that will allow us to take a stand when necessary and help us be unafraid to speak our minds and hearts, as we teach and touch others with our view of Judaism and the role of the Jewish people.

We all struggle to see the shadows that are hiding behind us. When finally we see them fullface, we can come to realize that they have always been a part of us. They simply have been waiting to become more integral to who we are as full persons.

The Creation of Eve from Adam's Rib: Reclaiming Our Complement

Although the first human being is pictured in Genesis Chapter One as originally having been both male and female, and subsequently divided in half, there is a second Creation story which stands in sharp contrast. In it, Eve is described as a separate entity: "The Lord God cast a deep sleep upon the man, and while he slept, [God] took one of his ribs and closed up the flesh at that spot. And the Lord God fashioned the rib *(tzeila)* that [God] had taken from the man into a woman, and [God] brought her to him." Though she was derived from Adam, Eve in fact was created independently of him. They were not simply two halves of one whole.

"The Lord God cast...
Genesis 2:21–22.

in several texts...
Bereshit Rabbah 17:6.

Most surprisingly, however, in several texts the rabbis understand the word *tzeila*, which is generally translated here as "rib," to mean rather "side," as it is used elsewhere in the Bible (e.g., Exodus 26:20). Even the famous early Alexandrian Jewish philosopher and teacher Philo shares the rabbis' understanding that Eve was one side of Adam. He stated that Eve was half of an original whole, having been created from one half of his body. Man and woman were parts of an original harmony which was split asunder.[5]

Since the word *tzeila* should be understood as "side" and not "rib," and the primal creation was one being that was split in two, it is clear that from the very outset of humankind's existence, there is a complete equality of men and women. They are forever to be seen as equal parts of one total conception of the human being. It then is the life quest of each side to be joined with its counterpart, recreating the lost wholeness. Each person seeks to return to primordial oneness, to integrate our different sides. This involves not only the male and female in us, but also the divine and human, and the good and evil.

This need for the integration of the human being's different "sides" is underscored in the Genesis text by Adam's response to his newly created partner. Seeing Eve for the first time and recognizing that she, unlike all the other creatures in the Garden, is like him in many ways, Adam blurts out: "This one at last is bone of my bones and flesh of my flesh. This one shall be called Woman (*Ishah*), for from Man (*Ish*) was she taken." Adam intuits that she is essentially like him; part of his very essence and being. (The Hebrew word for bone, *etzem*, can also mean "substance" or "essence".)

"This is the bone... Genesis 2:23.

Adam and Eve were indeed parts of the same original whole. Their very names, *Ish/Ishah*, underscore just how similar they were and are destined to become once again. "Hence a man leaves his father and mother, and clings to his wife and they shall be *basar echad*, one flesh," as they were when they were formed.

"Hence a man... Genesis 2:24.

This notion that every human being, each one of us,

[27]

though made up of different, sometimes conflicting forces, has the potential to achieve a greater wholeness, is evident from our text's well-known description of Eve as Adam's *ezer kenegdo*, as a helpmate for him. However, the term *neged* can have a negative connotation. It means "over against" or "opposite." Yet the word *neged* can also mean "close to," "parallel," or "equal to," as we see in many passages. (Note Esau's comment to Jacob following their rapprochement in Genesis 33:12.)

Ezer kenegdo...
Genesis 2:18.

It means "over...
See, in this regard, the usage in Genesis 21:16.

This dual meaning of *kenegdo* stresses, therefore, that Adam and Eve, though they represent contrasting forces, have the potential to be joined together once again. And in coming together, they will experience an even greater sense of unity than they did at the moment of creation since they will no longer be turned away from each other. The two opposites can indeed complement one another, and this potential is brought home in a comment by Rabbi Eleazer (4th century). In response to the question of why Eve is referred to as Adam's *ezer kenegdo*, he said that it comes to teach us that if Adam merits it, Eve will be a help (*ezer*) to him; but if he does not merit it, she will oppose him (*kenegdo*). The nature of their relationship is truly up to them.

in a comment...
B.T. Yebamot 63a. See also Bereshit Rabbah 17:3.

Eve, the other half of the primordial human being, is the sole creature capable of serving as an *"ezer kenegdo,"* of returning Adam to his original oneness. Although God proceeds to create all the animals and fowl in the hope of finding an appropriate mate for Adam, none suffices. This is not surprising since they are lesser beings than Adam. In fact, he names all these living creatures, demonstrating that they are subservient and in some ways even controlled by him. Contrastingly, we note how passive Adam is during the creation of the woman. He is in a deep sleep when God creates Eve from a part of him. He exercises absolutely no control over her existence; he does not even witness her birth. The result is that only the woman has the potential to function as his mate and complement him, since only she is his equal.[6]

Two Meant to Be One:
Recognizing Our Full Selves

The joining of the two sides will return us to the unity experienced at the beginning of creation in the Garden, when there was no distinction between male and female, Divine and human, good and evil. The world is not meant to witness eternally the separation between the two sides. This is clear from the words of our creation passage: "The Lord God said: 'It is not good *(lo tov)* for man to be alone.'" It indeed is not good for Adam to be alone, to stand apart from Eve, his other "side." The fragmented primal unity is not pleasing in God's eyes. This is brought home by the words *lo tov* (not good) that stand in tension with the phrase uttered by God following the creation of Adam and Eve in Chapter One: "And God saw all that God had made and it was very good *(tov me'od)*." You will recall that in this first Creation story, God made the human being in God's own image—unified; both male and female in one ("male and female God created them"). The human being can only be considered "very good" if the two opposing sides are joined together as one.[7]

This second story of creation in Chapter Two seems to strike a note of potential unity, when it states, "Hence a man leaves his father and mother, and clings to his wife, so that they become one flesh *(basar echad)*." However, that greater wholeness can only be achieved when one leaves his or her parents' home in search of the other side of self. Only leaving the safe confines of our youth, where we are cared for and protected, enables us to step up to our fuller maturity when we can struggle with our total selves and

"The Lord God said...
Genesis 2:18.

"And God saw...
Genesis 1:31.

"Hence a man...
Genesis 2:24.

reunite the disparate elements that are a part of us. Just as Adam and Eve had to leave the Garden of Eden to truly know each other, we are forced to leave behind the garden of our infancy. And then we will become *echad* (one); humankind will one day be "very good." The primal unity—Adam prior to the bifurcation into male/female, life/death, good/evil—will be recreated.

However, our creation story does not end with "oneness"; *echad* is not the final word. In the final verse of Chapter Two, following the phrase, "they shall be *one* flesh," we read:

"The two of them...
Genesis 2:25.

"The two of them were naked, the man and his wife, but they felt no shame." The writer highlights their differences and separateness—"the *two of them* were naked, the *man* and his *wife*." After noting their potential for unity, the text here emphasizes the distinctiveness and the tension between the two parts. As Adam and Eve are about to eat of the Tree of Knowledge, they become increasingly aware of their differences. As they stand naked facing each other for the very first time, astonished by how their bodies are shaped and recognizing their male-ness and female-ness, they are forced to cover themselves by making clothing out of fig leaves. The reality of their "otherness," though hidden, is now a fact of their lives.[8]

forced to cover...
Genesis 3:7.

The tension is not only between the male and female sides of the human being. Their eyes are opened to more than their physical differences. Listen to Genesis again: "God knows that as soon as you eat it, your eyes will be opened and you will...know good and evil....Then the eyes of both of them were opened and they perceived that they were naked."

"God knows that..
Genesis 3:5–7.

By eating the forbidden fruit, they also come to know the difference between good and evil. Adam and Eve are truly "naked" in the fullest sense of the term, having disobeyed God's command. Therefore, it is not surprising that Adam and Eve had to hide not only from one another, but also from God. As the idyllic unity of Eden fades, Adam conceals himself from the Divine, hiding as God's voice echoes through the Garden of Eden: "They heard the sound of the Lord God moving about in the Garden at the breezy time of the day; and the man and his wife hid from the Lord God among the trees of the Garden. The Lord God called out to the man and said to him, 'Where are you?' He replied, 'I heard the sound of You in the Garden, and I was afraid because I was naked, so I hid.'"

"They heard the sound...
Genesis 3:8–10.

God called out to Adam, asking whether he recognized his full self, that self made of both the Divine and human, male and female, and all Adam could do was shake with fear. He was not yet ready to come to grips with his other side.

Banishment East of Eden:
Our Search for Wholeness Begins

Wholeness is not to be achieved easily. The woman was indeed created from man's *tzeila*, his side, and she can potentially complement him, being an *ezer kenegdo*, a helpmate. Yet, the story of their eating of the fruit of the Tree of Knowledge makes it clear that Eve does not bring Adam to a greater sense of oneness. On the contrary, she is rather a stumbling block, an impediment.[9] As a result of their disobeying God, they stand apart from one another and in opposition to the Divine. They must leave the Garden of Eden. They must leave God's place precisely at the moment they seem quite God-like, when they possess a knowledge of good and evil: "And the Lord God said: 'Now that the human has become like one of us, knowing good and evil, what if he should stretch out his hand and take also from the Tree of Life and eat, and live forever.' So the Lord God banished him from the Garden of Eden, to till the soil from which he was taken. He drove the human out, and stationed the cherubim and

And the Lord God said...
Genesis 3:22–24.

[31]

the fiery ever-turning sword east of the Garden of Eden to guard the way to the Tree of Life."

They are banished from God's immediate presence to live in the imperfect world outside the Garden. They were returned to the earth, the *'adamah*, whence they were created, and their task was to cultivate it and to nurture themselves in the process.

The fact is that our primordial ancestors had to be separated from the Divine presence, just as the male and the female were separated in the Creation story, before they could be bonded together into an even more meaningful, lasting unity. The primal human being enjoyed unity at the outset of the Garden experience—a harmony between many sides, male/female, Divine/human and good/evil. Yet, true wholeness requires the struggle between the disparate elements.[10] True covenant between God and the human being cannot be sealed in the paradisial setting of the Garden of our infancy, but must come as a result of our experience in the world outside of Eden. To appreciate the very essence of oneness requires the experiencing of fragmentation, isolation, and loneliness.

So humankind is banished east of the Garden of Eden, *kedem le-Gan Eden*, in search of wholeness and integration. Adam and Eve move eastward, *kedmah*, a word which in Hebrew also means "preceeding," "earlier" or "origin." Humankind must move onward in order to return to its original, pristine state. Outside paradise, amidst the imperfection of this world, we human beings will discover a greater sense of our fuller selves, the male or female in us as well as our God-like natures. As we struggle desperately to overcome the aridity of the earth's soil outside the Garden, we begin to plant the seeds for our return. Our life journey is from the Garden of Eden, the *Gan Eden* of our infancy, to the Garden of our maturity, the messianic *Gan Eden*. It is there that the two sides of the primordial Adam will be fully reunified, facing each other, seeing each other and knowing one another. It is there that we will become one with that force we call God.

CHAPTER TWO

CAIN AND ABEL

The Conflict between Good and Evil

The story of Cain and Abel embodies basic concerns that all of us harbor, whether or not we have brothers or sisters. We are all caught up in the conflict between good and evil, and struggle with the question of why good deeds are not always recognized. This brief narrative presents us with our greatest challenges, especially the issue of the ability of human beings to radically change.

Cain, the fratricidal murderer, the farmer who is cut off from the earth and forced to be a ceaseless wanderer, in the end admits his guilt and repents. Because he does, God forgives him and pledges to protect him forever. Cain is every person: Human, vulnerable, sinful, even violent, yet he is able to grow. As he reconciles himself with his past and moves on, we too are forced to confront ourselves, our relationship with our siblings and parents, and with God. Can we make essential changes in ourselves, or are we destined simply to live out our lives as we are today? Do we have the ability to move beyond the inevitable pain of disappointments and rejection, and come to a greater sense of peace?

grandson Irad...
Genesis 4:18.

Just picture a very old Cain telling stories of his childhood to his grandson Irad, his son Enoch's only child. Irad asks his grandfather if he ever wished that he had a brother, to which Cain replies: "You don't know this, Irad, because I never speak about it. But once I did have a brother and his name was Abel." "What happened to him? Where does he live? Do you ever see him? How come you never talk about him, Grandpa?" As Irad peppered Cain with many questions, all that Cain could say in reply was that Abel died suddenly at a very young age and he really didn't remember much about him. With that, Cain changed the subject and began talking about how he had enjoyed helping his own father with the farming when he was a boy.

As we begin to explore the story of humankind outside the Garden of Eden, we like Cain are uncomfortable that our very first encounter is with the murder of Cain's brother Abel. Why at the outset of our human journey does the biblical writer force us to confront such a traumatic account of sibling rivalry, one ending in the violent taking of a human life? To respond to such an issue is very difficult, especially since Genesis Chapter Four is extremely terse. We are provided with only a sketchy narrative line and must fill in the missing details regarding the personalities of the brothers for ourselves.

To confront this challenging story of fratricidal murder, we must answer several perplexing questions. What is the nature of the relationship between Cain and Abel? Why did God pay attention to Abel's offerings and not to Cain's? What happened when the brothers confronted each other at the climax of the story? Did Cain ever regret the killing of his brother?

The Man Adam and His Wife Eve:
How Bonding with Another Bonds Us to God

Tantalizing questions such as these, as well as our concerns about the overriding message of this mythic story, invite us to respond personally and to struggle with what is clearly our own story. Even its opening words beckon us to immerse ourselves in the narrative: "And the Man knew his wife Eve and she conceived and bore Cain, saying: 'I have gained a male child with God's help'." Why does the story begin with the generic, "the Man" (*ha-Adam*), as opposed to the proper name, "Adam"? We expect the narrative to start with the words, "And Adam knew his wife Eve," but it doesn't. Perhaps because what is about to unfold, indeed the entire story of humankind outside the Garden of Eden, applies to every person, each and every one of us.

"And the man knew... Genesis 4:1.

The story embodies the basic concerns each human being harbors, whether or not he or she has brothers or sisters. We are all caught up in the conflict between good and evil, and wonder about reward and punishment and why good deeds are not always recognized. We, too, question whether people can radically change their behavior. And every set of parents struggles with its role and influence in rearing children. This haltingly brief account of Cain and Abel contains the most difficult humanistic and theological challenges. The text forces each of us to confront them by reminding us that these are not abstract issues but are our fundamental life questions.

We also cannot fail to note that the use of the impersonal term "the Man" in our verse stands in sharp contrast to the reference to the first Woman as "Eve" ("And the Man knew his wife Eve"). Adam's wife comes out of the Garden with a definite persona, while the Man must necessarily find his identity in the struggle of life outside Eden.[1] Only later, perhaps through the trauma he experienced with the loss

Only later... Genesis 4:12, 16.

of his first sons—the death of Abel and the banishment of Cain—does Adam gain both a greater degree of substance and self-awareness.

Is it any different for each of us? Haven't we gained a greater sense of ourselves, our strengths and weaknesses, when we have lived through moments of pain and anguish? Our own growth is often forged by life's most traumatic experiences—the loss of a job, separation and divorce, or the death of a someone close to us, whom we had loved inordinately. Realizing the strength that we possess, by surviving painful episodes in our lives, helps us to change and grow.

I think, for example, of my mother's death at a relatively young age due to cancer. Her extended suffering over several years, the physical pain she had to endure, and the toll it took on her, all were very difficult for me to witness. After all, I knew her to be a wonderfully warm, sensitive, and most giving person. She surely did not deserve what life had meted out to her. There were many moments that tested my faith as well as my emotional ability to endure her slow death. I could not understand why this had happened to her, of all people. During that difficult period, what I found most comforting was my study of Torah. It provided me with a grounding that allowed me to see things in a larger perspective. The worldview found in our traditional texts, which emphasizes the importance of each individual and the place of each in the continuum of the human experience, not only made me realize how much my mother had given to her family, but also buttressed my own strength to deal with this, or perhaps any tragedy.

The potential wholeness which human beings can achieve outside Eden is also highlighted by the choice of words in the first verse of the chapter: "And the Man knew (*yada*) his wife Eve."[2] Though clearly referring to the sexual act, the use of the Hebrew *yada*—he knew—implies some degree of intimacy and bonding between them. We can surely imagine what that first encounter must have been like, especially after their sheltered life in the Garden. Although they each had some idea of what the other was like from the time they spent together before their banishment from Eden, the moment they were joined as one was eye-opening for each of them. They recalled the moment of their creation when they were bound together, but seeing each other face to face as part of their embrace gave them an overwhelming sense of the lifeforce within them, and how they could draw upon it. Adam and Eve indeed "knew" each other as they had never known each other before. Just think! It is outside of paradise, amidst the struggle to survive, that they felt a closeness previously unknown, even in the Garden.

Perhaps in this light, the "expulsion" from the Garden of Eden is in reality a step up for humankind, a move towards greater maturity. No longer were Adam and Eve merely dependent upon God for their sustenance; no longer could they survive as two separate beings who bore no responsibility for their future. Outside the Garden they had to work together to insure survival, and in so doing they could come to a greater closeness and wholeness.

But this is not merely a mythic story of our first forebears. If we are honest with ourselves, we might admit that during the early years of our relationships with our spouses or significant others, years in which we struggled to make a go of it, when we had little material substance, we felt a closeness that we have found hard to sustain. Surrounded, even inundated by material provisions which many of us could not have imagined in our youth, it may be difficult to feel the once-so-tangible bonding and sharing.

The potential for bonding outside Eden is further stressed by Eve's comment after the birth of Cain. To be sure, Eve had witnessed the animals in the Garden giving birth to their young. She always watched with great interest as the mothers struggled through childbirth, and the sounds they made pierced her heart and mind. She could not help but wonder how it would feel if she were to birth her own child. She thought of this as she began to feel the child in her womb pushing downward as it reached towards life. And after what seemed like an eternity of pain, when she finally saw her baby emerge, she exclaimed, "I have gained *(kaniti)* an *ish*—a male child/a man—with God's help."[3]

"I have gained...
Genesis 4:1.

When Adam heard her, he was not at all sure what she meant. Her words were highly perplexing. When she used the word *ish*, he initially was sure that she was referring to him, since he was the only *ish*, the only man present. And since the verb *kanah* actually means "to purchase" or "to acquire," with the implication that the acquisition is forever, then Eve simply said, "Now that I have given birth to a male child, Adam and I are bound together forever. He is mine!" Adam immediately thought that when a woman sees that she has children, she feels that her husband is now her possession.[4] She, in effect, was telling Adam and us that Man and Woman, the two sides, can be bound together, integrated outside the Garden when they share in the acts of creation.

Eve simply said...
Bereshit Rabbah 22:2.

However, Adam then thought that perhaps Eve had meant something a bit different. For the verb *kaniti* can also mean "create," and then Eve would be saying, "I have created a male child."[5] Experiencing childbirth, Eve emphasized that in the moment of their union, they were God-like in their ability to procreate. They possessed the God-given ability to participate in the process of creation, and this could only happen outside of paradise. The God of creation, indeed, was present with Adam and Eve, for Eve adds: "I have gained (or created) a male child with God *(et Adonai)*." Their creative moment was suffused with God's presence. It was almost as if Eve really was saying, "I have gained (or solidified my relationship with) God in the process of birthing this child"—*kaniti...et Adonai*—Eve had

"I have gained...
See, in this regard, Bereshit Rabbah 22:2.

gotten hold of God!

In our lives we, too, can meld our human and Divine sides; like Adam and Eve, we can become one with the power we call God in the world. Any of us who have been blessed with children are acutely aware of the extraordinary feeling of God's presence at the moment of a child's birth. We know what the words *"et Adonai"* (with God) mean and what they say about potential oneness with God.

When our first child, Leora, was born in 1970, I distinctly remember standing outside the delivery room and feeling a tap on my shoulder. (In those "ancient days," fathers had not gained access to the birthing process.) A nurse motioned to an object she was carrying and said: "Mr. Cohen, here is your daughter." Looking down, I saw Leora for the first time, swaddled in a blanket and still covered with afterbirth, and realized probably for the first time the power that we human beings possess to act as creators. Screaming "It's a girl" at the top of my lungs (a substitute perhaps for: *"Kaniti isha et Adonai,"* I have created this miraculous, female child with God's help), I flew down five flights of stairs at Beth Israel Hospital in New York City, sensing God's presence in a way never before appreciated.

Years later, when reflecting on the moment of Cain's birth and the words uttered by Eve, Adam came to yet a third way of understanding what she meant when she blurted out, *"kaniti ish et Adonai"* (I have gotten a male-child with God)—that Eve saw their firstborn son as possessing a God-like quality. Cain was a human being with divine potential—an *ish et Adonai*; a creature with Godliness in him. She saw in her firstborn's image a certain celestial quality. This reading underscored for Adam their dual nature: God-like but utterly human at the very same time. (After all, it was the very same Cain who would bring death into the world through the killing of his brother!) Cain possessed two very distinct sides as every human being does.

a certain celestial...
See Pirkei d'Rabbi Eliezer, Chapter 21 and Midrash ha-Gadol to Genesis 4:1.

Abel, the Shadow of His Brother:
Becoming Aware of Our Other Side

"Eve then bore...
Genesis 4:2.

Abel is truly Cain's other side. Each time he is introduced into the narrative, all we are told about him is that he is "Cain's brother." When Abel is born, we learn that "[Eve] then bore his brother Abel." Even as we learn Abel's name, we hear of their relationship.

In addition, since there is no mention of a second conception, it is likely that Cain and Abel are twins. As two halves of one embryo, that Abel is defined solely in relationship to his "other side" is not surprising. His only identity is through his tie to Cain. In fact, Abel's very name in Hebrew, *Hevel*, indicates his lack of persona. Unlike Cain, the meaning of Abel's name is never explained. The word itself actually means "shadow," "wisp," or "vanity"; in essence, nothingness! Abel is just a shadow of his brother. Abel remains silent throughout the narrative and his appearance on the biblical stage is very brief. We never hear his voice; he never utters a word.

The fact that Abel is only a shadow of Cain is evident in the very different reactions to the two births by Eve. When Cain was born, Eve gave voice to the miracle of childbirth and the power of the moment for her as a parent: "I have gained a male-child with God's help." In contrast, when Abel, the second child appears, there is no fanfare, no self-reflection, no powerful moment of naming. The second birth is already quite commonplace. Abel appears almost as an afterthought; significant moments associated with him, like most second children, pale into insignificance. We today, as parents, similarly have fewer pictures, memorabilia, and even recollections of the births of our younger children. Perhaps Abel, too, suffered as a second child, needing more attention and stroking from his parents.

We, as readers, already can anticipate that the different

needs of the two brothers could engender conflict and struggle not uncommon even in our own families!

Different Personalities, Different Occupations: Being Shaped by Our Parents and Being Ourselves

After telling us about the birth of the brothers, the Genesis passage immediately identifies their occupations. Like most people today, the narrator seems more interested in the roles they play than in who they are. "Abel became a keeper of sheep while Cain became a tiller of the soil."

"Abel became a...
Genesis 4:2.

We cannot help but be struck by the stark contrast in the text, which seems to present us with the classic folkloristic confrontation between opposing forces. Their conflict also reflects the Temple cult and its sacrificial system. Animal sacrifices took priority over vegetable sacrifices. The brothers are indeed two sides that stand in conflict and the language itself of the text emphasizes the tension between the two: *"ve-Kayin hayah oved adamah"* (but Cain became a tiller of the soil).

Cain is very different from his brother Abel, even to the point of following in his father's footsteps and becoming a farmer. As in many of our families, one child enters the family business or emulates a parent professionally, no matter how difficult or incompatible the job is. In our biblical story, Cain tills the ground even though the land was cursed because Adam had disobeyed God's command in the Garden. Doing so only compounded Adam's sin. The irony, of course, is that the farmer and the shepherd are utterly dependent upon each other for their survival. One supplies the food necessary, while the other provides the wool and skins for protection. The two brothers, who seem so different, are nevertheless umbilically tied to one another.

the land was cursed...
See Genesis 3:17.

But we might honestly wonder what role their parents played not only in their work choices, but in shaping who they became? And even more to the point, where are Adam and Eve during this time? So much is left out of the story that we haven't the faintest notion of Adam and Eve's involvement in their sons' lives. Does the silence about Adam and Eve tell us something of the lack of their influence? If only the parents could share with us their perceptions of their two boys.

the slaying of Abel...
See *The Life of Adam and Eve,* an early compilation which is part of the Apocrypha.

It is possible to imagine that the slaying of Abel by Cain did not come as a wholly unexpected event to his parents. In a dream, Eve saw the blood of Abel on the hands of Cain and woke up with a start. When she told Adam of her dream, he responded lamentingly, "May this not portend the death of Abel at the hand of Cain!" So what did these two good parents do? As we would, they separated the two boys, assigning to each a place of his own and teaching them different occupations. Cain became a tiller of the earth, while Abel became a keeper of sheep. But all the parents' efforts failed. In spite of everything Adam and Eve did, that day in the field Cain rose up and slew his brother Abel.

Why should we exonerate Adam and Eve so easily? Were they not in part responsible for what happened, since if they had been present, the moment of violence and tragedy might have been avoided? It would seem that this is an important lesson about ourselves as parents. What is stressed is that we should not inappropriately bear the guilt and burden of our children's actions. No matter what parents do for their children or how much direction they may impart, in the end, we are our own persons and responsible for our actions. Cain killed his brother Abel, and probably would have even if Adam and Eve had been model parents!

The Brothers' Offerings:
Giving the Best We Have and Being Rejected

The contrast between Cain and Abel, the two sides of one

embryo, is further accentuated by the offerings each made and God's response to them: "In the course of time, Cain brought an offering to the Lord from the fruit of the soil; and Abel also brought from the choicest of the firstlings of his flock. The Lord paid heed to Abel and his offering, but to Cain and his offering [God] paid no heed." The question that readers in every generation have asked is, why did God accept Abel's and reject Cain's sacrifice? For many, the reason is clear: Abel brought the firstlings of his flock; he in effect chose the best that he had.[6] The text emphasizes this by saying that Abel brought "from the firstlings of *his* flock." Therefore, "God paid attention *to Abel* and to his offering." We understand the contrast. Cain took whatever fruit or vegetables were available, with no thought as to their quality—a turnip from here, a sad looking apple from there. He did not bring the choicest. That is why Cain is compared to a bad tenant farmer who eats of the first ripe figs, but presents the king with the late figs. As a result, God had no use for Cain's gifts.

"In the course of time...
Genesis 4:3–5.

he in effect...
Bereshit Rabbah 22:5.

That is why...
Bereshit Rabbah 22:5.

From this perspective, we are no different than Cain. We, too, generally give perfunctorily to important charities thereby assuaging our consciences. Almost as if by rote, we write checks at the end of the calendar year for the same small amounts to the charities that appeal to us. Yet, we know we are capable of giving much more. True giving can only occur if we stretch ourselves a bit, rather than sending in a check for a nominal amount just so we can say that we contributed. Of course, all of us must prioritize our giving, which in itself is quite difficult. However, when like Abel we give the best that we have and the most that we can, we know in our hearts that we have fulfilled our obligation.

But we cannot help thinking that to contrast the two brothers in this manner is grossly unfair. After all, remember what our text actually says: "In the course of time, Cain brought an offering to the Lord from the fruit of the soil;

and Abel also brought from the choicest of the firstlings of his flock." If we put ourselves in Cain's place, we can imagine his reaction to God's response to the offerings. Listen to his voice: "I cannot believe what's happened! I was the one who brought an offering to God. I acted voluntarily. I was the first to bring a sacrifice. My father had never been asked to set aside an offering in the Garden of Eden. Only outside the Garden, caught up in the struggle to survive, I was the one who felt moved to bring a gift in order to recognize God's presence in the world and my relationship with the Divine."

Cain is right! What indeed is most interesting about all this is that the sacrifices seem to be Cain's idea. The text simply states: "And Abel also brought"—*Ve-Hevel hayvi gam hu*. The words *gam hu* (he also) indicate that Cain initiated the offerings. Abel learned what was expected and imitated his brother. This only added fuel to Cain's response to God's recognition of Abel's offering. Further venting, this time to his brother, Cain angrily says to Abel: "You had no intention of bringing anything at all until you found out what I was going to offer. You were jealous and so you went out and got all these animals together to make sure that you would not be outdone." The point to be stressed here is that even when they are most distinguished and contrasted, the brothers seem to act in a similar manner. They mirror and compete with one another, as children in a family often do.

One classic example of modern midrash that underscores the fact that Abel simply learned what was expected from his older brother and then outdid him comes in a crucial scene in John Steinbeck's *East of Eden*. Adam is portrayed as a California farmer struggling to meet the mortgage payments during World War One. At a Thanksgiving celebration, Caleb, who has saved two thousand dollars by trading commodities sold in Europe, presents his father with the money in order to help him keep the farm. Adam's volatile

"And Abel also...
Genesis 4:4.

"You had no intention...
Keli Yakar to Genesis 4:3, which is the source for Cain's words here.

response to Caleb's gift, which Adam described as "filthy lucre," since it was earned by taking advantage of the wartime situation, leaves Caleb speechless and utterly devastated. Aaron, who is standing on the side and witnessing the interaction, comes forward to announce that he has become engaged to be married. Aaron knew how to please his father.[7] "And Abel also brought...an offering."

Each of us knows this moment, whether as parents or as children, or both. It happens to each of us lucky enough to have more than one child, when we are moved to respond negatively to a gesture of one of our children, from which another learns a seemingly more appropriate expression. Some ten years ago, when our children were quite young, at the family's celebration of my birthday, our son Ilan, then about seven, came up and handed me a white envelope, saying, "Here's your present, Dad. I couldn't think of anything to get you, so I'm giving you the money I saved." I opened the envelope and found five single dollar bills, which represented his allowance for several weeks. Though surely not meaning to hurt his feelings, I thoughtlessly berated him, saying, "Ilan, it isn't appropriate for a child to give his parent money as a birthday present." As he walked away with tears rolling down his cheeks, his sister Mali, standing off to the side, rushed to her room, only to return momentarily holding a picture. She gave it me and said that she drew the picture in art class for my birthday. Though it was difficult to tell just what the nature of her masterpiece was, I kissed her and told her how much I appreciated the gift. It is easy to imagine what went through Ilan's mind at that moment, perhaps feelings similar to Cain's, who only wanted to please his father by giving a gift he thought his father would cherish. Like Cain, all Ilan wanted to do was show his affection for his father in his own way.

In this light, we should also keep in mind that the text never says that Cain sinned. All we are told is that Cain

All we are told is...
Genesis 4:4–5.

brought an offering, that Abel followed suit, and that God paid attention to Abel's offering, but not to Cain's.[8] There is no implied value judgment here; no notion of acceptance or rejection by God. Cain is not accused of any wrongdoing in our Genesis text; all that he can be accused of is that he gave something of himself.

Perhaps in fact the rejection is only the result of Cain's perception or feelings; the reaction of an older sibling who is jealous when his parent pays attention to a brother or sister for the first time. Do we really think the value of the offerings mattered that much to God? God might simply have responded to the two individuals and their needs, as the text indicates by mentioning the brothers' names first and then their offerings: "The Lord paid heed *to Abel* and to his offering, but *to Cain* and to his offering [God] paid no heed." Like any parent with more than one child, God may have decided that Abel needed affirmation, given his position vis a vis his brother. After all, Abel was born after Cain's appearance and little fuss was made of him. All of us, parents and children, know this moment. We have experienced it from both sides: The pain of rejection as children, though perhaps never intended by our parents, and the uneasiness of trying to respond to the needs of all our own children. This is especially poignant for those of us who live in blended families and struggle every day to provide our different children with what they so desperately need. Will our responses to an individual child ever be totally appreciated or even understood?

Cain's Real Test:
How Do We Respond to Adversity?

"Cain was much...
Genesis 4:5

All that the biblical writer tells us of Cain's reaction to God's paying attention to Abel are the following terse words: "Cain was much distressed and he was crestfallen."

[48]

Can this be the extent of Cain's reaction to God's seeming rejection of his offering? If only Cain could talk to us, he would probably have said: "I have been wronged. I believed that the world was created through goodness, but now I see that good deeds are not rewarded. God rules the world with an arbitrary power. Why else would God respect Abel's offering and not mine?"

"I have been wronged...
The Palestinian Targum to Genesis 4:8

So how shall we respond to Cain, who perceived that his offering had been unjustifiably rejected? Why did God pay attention to Abel's sacrifice, ignoring Cain's voluntary gift? There may be no adequate answer that we can give to Cain; no way to mollify his anguish. Perhaps the biblical writer is communicating to the generations of readers who have turned to the Bible for a sense of the meaning and purpose of life the most important lesson about living outside the Garden. In our inability to respond to Cain's plea for an explanation, we learn that life in the real world as we experience it is fraught with inequities and unanswerable questions. There simply is no guarantee that good deeds are rewarded, that sacrifices are always going to be appreciated. Life outside the Garden of Eden is one of struggle to live without any clear answers. Each of us in our lives is asked to live with adversity, pain, and misfortune. The clear challenge in this regard is how to live with ambivalence and uncertainty.

The only thing we can ask of Cain at this point, and by extension ourselves, is whether he (or we) can handle the seeming rejection and move beyond it. Does he have the strength to reconcile himself to the consequences of what he has done? Can he overcome the distance between himself and his brother, between himself and God and move to a greater sense of wholeness and unity? This is the essence of his test.

In responding to Cain's expression of anguish, God does indeed challenge him in no uncertain terms to face his

"Why are you distressed...
Genesis 4:6–7.

situation squarely and deal with the adversity. God asks Cain: "Why are you distressed and why are you so crestfallen? If you will do well, there will be uplift. But if you do not do well, sin lurks at the door; its urge is toward you, but you can control it." God's words can be understood as a chastisement of Cain; God seemingly chides Cain by telling him that he got what he deserved—"had you done well, you would have been rewarded." Such an interpretation of our verse sees God's words as a comment upon what Cain has already done.

However, they are better understood not as a recollection of past action, but rather a present and future challenge: "If you do well, there will be uplift." God in effect is saying to Cain, "What is done, is done. Where do you go from here?"[9] Cain is told that he has the power not only to control his reactions, but to deal with adversity. If he will respond well, God will forgive him. (Here the word *seyt* (uplift) from the root *nasa* is understood to mean "forgive.") Cain is given a second chance. How will he react?

If he will respond...
Bereshit Rabbah 22:6.

Cain's reaction comes in the ensuing conversation with Abel: "Cain said to his brother Abel...when they were in the field, and Cain set upon his brother and killed him."

"Cain said to his...
Genesis 4:8.

When God asked Cain why he was so distressed, Cain either chose not to or simply could not respond. Instead of expressing his hurt and anger to God, the proverbial parent and the appropriate object of his feelings, he kept them inside.[10] It is not clear how long Cain's feelings of rejection festered within. But this much we do know: Cain is next pictured speaking to his brother. What exactly the circumstances were and what he said are not recorded.[11]

The glaring gap in the text ("Cain said to his brother Abel...when they were in the field") demands that each reader fill in the missing words. If it were Cain who went out to the field in which Abel was grazing his sheep, what was his purpose? Was it simply that Cain was reaching out to the only one he could, to his brother, for sympathy and support? Perhaps all Cain wanted was someone to talk to in order to unburden himself. He desperately needed a brother who could be his ally.[12] Or did an angry, vindictive Cain go looking for the object of his jealousy? Perhaps he needed to vent his pent-up emotions on his brother, the one closest to him, his other half.

If we are honest with ourselves, we in fact know what Cain said to Abel that day in the field, since we have had that very conversation with our own sibling(s) many times. We, like Cain, have felt rejected by our parents and have sought consolation from a brother or sister, or an opportunity to give vent to an angry accusation. We know that moment. We have lived it, as have our children, though we—like the biblical writer—would rather not fill in the words. It might be too painful. Silence is a better option for all concerned.

Whatever Cain's intent was in confronting his brother, there is no response from Abel. He does not break his silence. Is the ellipsis intentional on the part of the biblical writer, indicating to us that Abel simply was not there when Cain needed him the most? Does Abel therefore bear some of the responsibilty for what ultimately happened? Could he not have helped avoid the tragedy by responding to his brother's pain? It is interesting that Cain and Abel, who are pictured as complete opposites—shepherd and farmer, aggressive and passive, evil and innocent—act in a similar manner at the crucial moment: They both remain silent. Cain does not respond to God and Abel does not speak to Cain. The brothers seem to be bound together in their silence and perhaps even in their guilt!

It is not surprising that Cain and Abel who are so different would occasionally act in a similar manner. We would expect this from twins who are two sides of a whole; sometimes mirrors of each other. In fact, when Cain kills Abel, it is as if Cain has imitated his brother's animal sacrifice. Abel, in his death, is not only identified with his own sacrifice, the animals from his flock, but he becomes Cain's animal sacrifice as well.[13] In a pastoral age in which animal sacrifices were primary, both brothers brought a shepherd's offering.

The unnecessary sacrifice could have been avoided if only Cain could have voiced his anger to God and released some of his terrible feeling of rejection, and if Abel could somehow have found words to console his older brother. The two brothers either did not hear or could not speak, and we shudder at the harsh reality of what ensued: "Cain set upon his brother Abel and killed him." Chastised by his "parent" and ignored by his brother, Cain was moved to a point of utter anguish, frustration, and isolation. At that moment, unable to control his emotions, as God had urged, Cain lashed out at his brother. The biblical writer emphasizes the relationship by reminding us no less than five times in three verses that Abel was Cain's brother.

no less than five times...
See Genesis 4: 8–10.

In killing Abel, Cain actually killed a part of himself. That Cain was also a victim is dramatically underscored in a tradition describing Eve's reaction upon learning of Abel's death at Cain's hands. Listen to Eve's startling words; she cannot decide whom to mourn more: "Two sorrows have come upon wretched me in a single day; two blows have befallen me in a single hour. If I turn my eyes to the ground, the corpse of the slain one gives me pain, and if I raise my eyes, then I see this one shaking and trembling. I do not know which of them I should lament; I know not for which of the two I should weep."[14]

"Two sorrows have come...
This legend is taken from Symmachus' *Life of Abel*, an early Syriac text.

Cain's Last Chance:
Can We Accept Responsibility for Our Actions?

Cain is once again confronted by God, who, as Abel lies dead in the dust beside him, asks him: "Where is your brother Abel?" The omnipresent and omniscient Divine surely knows what has happened. God does not have to ask any questions. This is simply a final opportunity for Cain to acknowledge his act; to bear responsibility for what he did by responding openly to God's question. Unfortunately, he fails the test.

Cain is evasive: "I do not know," he replies, "Am I my brother's keeper?"

"I do not know...
Genesis 4:9.

It is painful to see just how far human beings have moved apart. You will recall that our story began with the text telling us that "the Man knew *(yada)* his wife Eve," implying a degree of intimacy and bonding. Here, Cain has neither knowledge of what has transpired, nor what was expected of him in relation to his brother. He proclaims: *"Lo yadati,"* either to be translated, "I do not know" or "I did not know that [I am my brother's keeper]." In either case, at this point there was no real connection between them, or at least Cain was not able to recognize one.

the Man knew...
Genesis 4:1.

Perhaps Cain was pleading ignorance in the hope of convincing God that he was innocent. But how could he expect that God would accept the argument? Should he not have known that brothers have responsibilities toward one another? That whether in a society or family, people are expected to know how to act and what is appropriate behavior?

Cain's real sin is his inability to recognize his responsibility toward his brother and for his own actions, and to admit his guilt. Cain does respond, but he does not acknowledge that he bears any guilt at all for the death of his brother, his other side. He cannot admit that had he acted differently, Abel would still be alive. Cain did have the power to preserve his brother's life; he was his "keeper," his *shomer.* Cain could have acted in God's stead, sustaining life, as indicated by his use of the term *anochi,* which generally is found when God is speaking in the first person. Cain ironically asks the question of God: "Am I *(anochi)* my brother's keeper?"—as if unconsciously to underscore his true power, which is not realized in this scene. Cain fails to recognize his other side, either his brother or his own God-like potential.

It could even be worse. Perhaps Cain, when he proclaims: "Am I *(anochi)* my brother's keeper?" is really challenging God and God's role in the episode. By recognizing that the word *anochi* is a term used in relationship to God and by reversing the syntax, Cain could be declaring that God is guilty: "God *(Anochi)* is my brother's keeper!" Just listen to Cain's argument. When God said to Cain, "Where is your brother Abel?", Cain replied: "I do not know. Am I my brother's keeper? You are the power that holds watch over all your creatures, yet you demand account of me?" And then he drives home his argument with an artful analogy to the case of a thief who stole vessels at night and was not caught. In the morning, the watchman apprehended him and accused him of stealing the previous night. The thief said in reply: "It is true that I am a thief, but I simply did that which I am accustomed to doing. On the other hand, you are a watchman by profession and you did not fulfill your responsibilities. My job is to steal and yours to prevent me from stealing. If I succeeded, whose fault is it?" So, too, Cain said to God: "You are the keeper and preserver of all things, yet you allowed me to kill my brother and even created within me the evil inclination. You are the real murderer!"[15]

Cain's defense here is a familiar one. The individual who is unwilling to assume any responsibility for his or her actions blames parents, siblings, societal problems, or almost anything else for what he or she has done. We have heard the claim that "the devil made me do it" all too often. And that is precisely the point of our story: Cain's inability to understand what was expected of him and to recognize that

Listen to Cain's argument...
Midrash Tanhuma ha-Nidpas, *Bereshit* #9.

he did something terribly wrong.

Cain's Punishment of Self-alienation: Sinning Means Losing a Part of Ourselves

After Cain fails to take responsibility for his actions, God said to him: "What have you done? Your brother's blood cries out to me from the ground." The omniscient Divinity surely knows what has transpired; the question is clearly rhetorical. By asking, "What have you done," God gives expression to our horror over what transpired: Both the killing of Abel and Cain's inability to bear responsibility for the act. But then God adds the words "the sound (or voice) of your brother's blood cries out to me from the ground." What in the world does this mean?

"What have to done...
Genesis 4:10.

First, there is a powerful irony here. Abel never speaks in the entire narrative, but his blood cries out! Indeed, his silence speaks volumes at this juncture.[16] Abel, the other side of Cain, his shadow, finally emotes and becomes a presence in death which he was not while he was alive. His voice cries out to God from the ground (the *adamah*), "which opened its mouth to receive [his] blood *(dam)*," his life force.

"which opened its mouth...
Genesis 4:11.

In this light, it is also interesting that the previous mention of the word *kol,* voice or sound, is found in the preceding chapter of Genesis, following the eating of the fruit of the Tree of Knowledge: "[Adam and Eve] heard the sound *(kol)* of God moving about in the Garden [of Eden]." There, God's voice booms forth with the divine accusation, "Where are you?" as the first humans hide from the Divine.

"Adam and Eve heard...
Genesis 3:8.

So, too, in our story, the sound of the life force in Abel, the divine in him, cries out accusingly, calling for retribution. And whence does the voice emanate? It calls forth from the *adamah,* the earth, the place of limitation and death (since the earth has been cursed). The divine in the human being calls out; our other side, that which is God-like in us, must be heard.

And God does hear, and responds by spelling out Cain's punishment: "Therefore, you shall be banished from the ground, which opened its mouth to receive your brother's blood from your hand. If you till the soil, it shall no longer yield its strength to you. You shall become a ceaseless wanderer on the earth."

Therefore you shall be...
Genesis 4:11–12.

Like his father Adam, Cain is cursed through the ground, though Cain's punishment is more severe. Adam was forced to work the land with the sweat of his brow, and only through much effort would he draw food from the earth. But the earth would no longer sustain his son. Cain, the farmer, was cut off from the land. Cain was banished from the soil which had sustained him as a farmer.[17]

Cain's punishment is clear: He is cut off from the source of his very being, that which defines his existence. Cain killed Abel and, as a result, he experienced self-alienation; he lost a part of himself.

In killing his brother, he became his brother: Cain, the sedentary farmer, killed Abel, the wandering shepherd, and he himself becomes a wanderer! Cain had internalized the other side of himself; he was relegated to carrying it with him for the rest of his life. According to a legend that circulated among the people, the dog which had been Abel's constant companion and which helped Abel tend his flock, now was seen guarding and protecting Cain.

According to a legend...
Bereshit Rabbah 22:13.

Some even say that Cain, in becoming Abel, shared his brother's fate. He, too, was murdered by a blood relative. Although there is no actual mention of Cain's death in the Bible and he simply fades from the biblical drama after settling down and raising a family, the rabbis imagine that Cain was killed by Lamech, who lived five generations later.[18] In fact, Cain is described as having killed his brother Abel by striking him with a stone, and in turn was killed himself when Lamech struck him with a stone.

the rabbis imagine...
See Midrash Tanhuma ha-Nidpas, *Bereshit* #11.

having killed his...
The *Book of Jubilees* 4:31 and Aggadat *Bereshit*, Chapter 26.

Seemingly the upshot of the fratricide is clear: The killing of Abel meant the death of Cain as well. The brothers suffered the same end, which is to be expected given their bonding. Cain and Abel could be compared to two trees standing next to each other. When a strong wind came and uprooted one, it fell upon the other and uprooted it. In a figurative sense, both Cain and Abel died that fateful day in the field.

Cain and Abel could be...
Bereshit Rabbah 23:5.

Cain—the Symbol of Repentance: How We Can Accept Responsibility and Change

Yet, even though Cain was eventually to share Abel's fate because of his brutal crime, could the rabbis deny him the possibility of repenting for his sins? Given their stress on the human being's potential for change and God's desire that we return, how could they close off the hope of future generations for renewal by shutting the door of repentance to Cain? Indeed, they believed and constantly emphasized that the gates of repentance are always open, ever beckoning each of us to enter.

gates of repentance...
See, for example, Eichah Rabbah 3:44.

Yet the reader will surely ask: Even if Cain were given the chance, would he have the strength and desire to change? Could he admit his guilt and ask for forgiveness? Could he reconcile himself to what he had done, and thereby enable himself to move on with his life?

All we are left with in this regard are Cain's final words of response to the punishment which God had pronounced upon him. Cain said to God: "My punishment is too great to bear! Since You have banished me this day from the soil, and I must avoid Your presence and be a restless wanderer on the earth, anyone who meets me may kill me."

Cain said to God...
Genesis 4:13–14.

At first glance Cain's words, "My punishment is too great to bear," imply that he does not have the strength to survive his banishment from the soil, becoming a fugitive and a wanderer. Almost all English translations of the Bible understand Cain's response in this way.[19]

But the midrashic process demands that we pay attention to every word, to every detail. A close reading of the Hebrew here is crucial, since Cain actually says: "*Gadol avoni mi-neso,*" my *avon* is too great to bear. Although the Hebrew term avon can mean "punishment" in the Bible, it very rarely does. In almost all cases it means "sin," which would cast Cain's words in a very different light. Reading in this manner, as the rabbis in the Tradition consistently do, we witness a very different Cain here. Finally, after God had given him several opportunities to take responsibility for what he had done, Cain utters the words "my sin." The arrogance is gone and all we are left with is a vulnerable, contrite Cain who is willing to admit his failure.

as the rabbis...
Targum Yerushalmi to Genesis 4:10, Vayiqra Rabbah 10:5, and Pirkei d'Rabbi Eliezer, Chap. 21.

this recreation of...
Bereshit Rabbah 22:11.

Listen to this recreation of Cain's words: "My sin is surely greater than my father's sin. My father transgressed a very minor precept and, as a result, was expelled from the Garden of Eden. If I transgressed the most serious prohibition, murder, what shall be my punishment?" Cain clearly recognizes the seriousness of what he has done. But there is more. Cain's words are understood as a plea to God for forgiveness. This is based not only upon reading his words as a supplication, but also understanding the word *mi-neso* not as "to bear," but rather as "to be forgiven."[20] In this light, Cain pleads with God: "Is my sin too great to be forgiven?" Cain cannot 'bear' his sin by himself; he needs God to help him. He recognizes that human beings cannot survive alone in this world; survival and uplift can only come through relationship with God. And so Cain is even pictured as actually praying to God for forgiveness. Imagine him saying: "Master of the universe, you bear the whole world, and yet my sin you will not bear. You yourself have written: '[Who is like God] who pardons iniquity and forgives transgression' [Micah 7:18]. Pardon my sin for it is great."

Imagine him saying...
Devarim Rabbah 8:1, Midrash Lekah Tov to Genesis 4:12 and Bereshit Rabbah 97(NV).

It is his willingness to admit his guilt before God that impels the rabbis to see Cain as the primary model of repentance. Cain, the brutal murderer who consistently denies any responsibility, is transformed into a symbol of change, from which all of us can learn. Cain's repentance even had an impact upon his father. Many years later, Adam encounters Cain and hardly recognizes him. He says: "Cain, is that you? What happened to you? I thought God killed you after you murdered Abel." Cain replied to his father: "No, I repented and God forgave me!" Thereupon, Adam began to beat his face and he lamented: "So great is the power of repentance and I did not know it." At that moment, Adam arose and composed a hymn of praise to God, beginning with the words, "It is a good thing to confess [your sins] unto the Lord."[21]

Many years later... See Bereshit Rabbah 22:13 as well as Pesikta d'Rav Kahana 24:1 and Midrash ha-Gadol to Genesis 4:16.

Adam now understood that the potential for change and forgiveness is ever present and we, like Cain, can grow and move towards a higher vision of ourselves. Cain is every person: Human, vulnerable, sinful, even violent, yet he can change. By recognizing what he has done, and accepting his fate, he has reconciled himself with the past and can now move on. The conclusion in the rabbinic reading of the narrative is that Cain, of all the biblical characters, is the embodiment of *Teshuvah* (Repentance)!

But do we believe that people can essentially change? Is it possible for us, as it was for Cain, to shed past actions and become a new person? Or in our heart of hearts do we know that all the good intentions we have each year as we take stock of ourselves merely remain good intentions? We are who we are; people don't change, just as leopards do not change their spots. Do we recite our confessional prayers (as Jews on Yom Kippur, for instance) merely by rote, or do we have confidence that if we work hard at it, we can reach towards our highest selves? Cain challenges us and our belief in ourselves. Hearing his words ("My sin is too great to bear"), we have no choice but to take an honest look at ourselves and ask whether we must remain who we are today. Are we destined to merely play at any attempt to change our ways of acting and treating others?

God becomes Cain's Protector:
The Divine Never Abandons Us

The fact that Cain's repentance resulted in God's forgiving him is immediately evident in the Divine's response to Cain's fear that as a wanderer he would meet certain death: "The Lord said to him: 'I promise, if anyone kills Cain, sevenfold vengeance shall be taken on him.'" And the Lord put a mark on Cain, lest anyone who meets him should kill him. God, who had been Cain's accuser and judge, now seems to become his protector. God's attribute of mercy is very much in evidence and the tone with which the Divine relates to Cain is different. Once he has acknowledged his sin, he becomes reconciled with the Divine. God becomes the concerned parent who will do everything in his power to protect his child and insure his survival. The change from the outset of the narrative is startling. The God who chastised Cain, saying: "What have you done? Your brother's blood cries out to me from the ground," now pledges to defend Cain and punish those who would harm him! God says: "If anyone kills Cain, sevenfold vengeance shall be taken on him" and the Hebrew word for "shall be taken upon him" is simply *"yukam."* The very same Hebrew root described Cain rising up and killing Abel earlier in the story (Genesis 4:8): "And he rose up *(va-yakom)* against his brother Abel and killed him." The message therefore is clear: Cain rose up *(yakom)* and killed his brother, and God punished him. Now God will raise up *(yukam)* vengeance on those attacking Cain!

An even more obvious indication that Cain now had a

"The Lord said to him...
Genesis 4:15.

"What have you done...
Genesis 4:10.

divine protector was the mark God placed upon him. Many commentators over the centuries, viewing Cain negatively throughout the biblical narrative, understood the mark as a brand that labels Cain as a murderer rejected by the Divine. According to them, Cain, the wanderer, bears the sign of the outcast. However, the Hebrew term used for "mark" here is the word *ot* which is used in the Bible as a sign of covenant with God.[22] The mark shows us that Cain stood in renewed relationship with God. The utterly fragile human being who had the capacity to kill now was in God's charge as he started on the second part of his life's journey.[23]

The Aftermath:
Affirming Our Potential for Goodness

"Cain left the presence of the Lord and settled in the land of Nod, east of Eden. Cain knew his wife, and she conceived and bore Enoch. And [Cain] founded a city and named the city after his son." According to God's expressed punishment, Cain was to become a fugitive and wanderer, and indeed he is forced to leave God's presence. Like his father before him, when Adam was banished from the Garden of Eden, Cain travels eastward.[24] He, too, is cut off from Eden, his roots, even from the Divine it seems, and he settles in the land of Nod, which in Hebrew means "wandering" or "restlessness." Ostensibly, nowhere could Cain find rest and mooring.

> "Cain left the...
> Genesis 4:16–17.

However, we are surprised to learn that Cain settles down in the land of Nod. He is not portrayed as a wanderer; far from it. Cain dwells in one place and begins to raise a family and even builds a city! What happened to God's judgment and the punishment he was to suffer? Cain was condemned to be a wanderer forever, yet he clearly prospers and flourishes during his lifetime. Cain, the repentant sinner who was accepted back by God, not only was able to move beyond the murder of his brother, but succeeded in putting his life back together.

In this story of rejection, violence and change, Cain challenges each of us to recognize who we are and what we can become. It is the tension between Cain and Abel, and the human and divine in each of us, that must be reconciled if we are to move back to or forward from the Garden of Eden. The conflict between Cain and Abel was irreconcilable—Cain killed his younger brother. Yet Cain did grow and mature, and though he carried the burden of his actions his entire life, he also bore the sign of the covenant, of relationship with God. At the end of the saga, there is an affirmation of potential goodness in the world and in each of us, and our ability to achieve wholeness.[25]

"Adam knew his..."
Genesis 4:25.

That affirmation is seen not only in Cain's repentance and later success, but also in Adam and Eve's response to the tragic loss of their son, Abel: "Adam knew his wife again, and she bore a son and named him Seth, meaning God has provided me with another offspring in place of Abel, for Cain had killed him." Their first act in the face of death was to conceive another child. Seth's birth signified that life can be good and relationships meaningful, even if fraught with pain and sorrow. Seth took Abel's place. Though Abel, Cain's twin and his other half, had died, it was as if he were still alive. The line of descent from Adam and Eve would follow the younger son. However, the fact that Seth stood in Abel's stead also insured that the struggle between the two sides was transmitted to the next generation.

We, like Cain, may have taken small steps toward a sense of our higher selves by admitting our frailty and recognizing who we are, yet our inner struggle continues. The Eden of our dreams seems like a lifetime away.

CHAPTER THREE

ISHMAEL AND ISAAC

The Tensions between Siblings

Life in Abraham's family was fraught with ongoing turmoil. For all of his successes as a clan chieftain in Canaan and his ability to protect and defend others, his relationships with his own kin left much to be desired. Abraham struggled to live in peace with Lot, his nephew, just as later he would be torn apart by the difficult interactions among his wives and sons.

Abraham must have suffered greatly when Hagar and Ishmael were banished to the desert, when on Mt. Moriah he almost took the life of his precious Isaac, and when he had to bury Sarah upon his return without Isaac. These events left him alone in the world, bereft of all that was dear to him. The story of Abraham's family raises many difficult questions with which we ourselves struggle. Was it too late for Abraham to find personal happiness and is it too late for us within our own families? Can Isaac and Ishmael ever come together and can their descendants find a way of living together in peace? Can siblings overcome years of separation and embrace once again?

Abraham stood at the opening to his tent for a very long time as he watched Hagar and Ishmael slowly making their way out of the camp. Seeing his son disappear over the next hill as Ishmael and his mother headed into the wilderness of Beersheba and realizing that he probably would never see Ishmael again, Abraham began to shudder. Although the sun already was quite high in the morning sky and the desert heat beat down upon him, Abraham felt chilled as tears rolled down his cheeks. He could not help but think how his son must feel being sent away from his father's house, the house he had lived in for all of his thirteen years. And as he recoiled with the pain that he had caused Ishmael, Abraham began to recall his own journey from his father's house, his own feelings of loneliness and isolation.

Ishmael and his mother... Genesis 21:14.

From the very outset of Abraham's journey from Ur, he experienced a sense of separation from his family. Though one of three sons born to Terah, he alone accompanied his father as they set off for Haran. His brother Haran seems to have died earlier in Ur, and his second sibling, Nahor, was left behind for no apparent reason. Nahor's absence is underscored by the fact that Lot, the son of the deceased Haran, was a part of the entourage.[1] Why did Terah not take Nahor and his immediate family with the clan? Abraham thought of his brothers as he strained to see Ishmael and Hagar in the distance.

one of three sons... Genesis 11:27–31.

Abraham and Lot Separate: Why Do Families Fall Apart?

Now that he had lost Ishmael forever, Abraham remembered the day that his nephew Lot left Beersheba, travelled eastward and settled in the plain of the Jordan River near the cities of Sodom and Gemorrah. Lot's departure was very difficult for Abraham, since he thought of him more as a brother or son, than a nephew. He was the one remaining

Lot left Beersheba... Genesis 13:9–11.

familial link to Abraham's past. After Abraham's father Terah died and Abraham left Haran for the Land of Canaan as God had commanded him, Lot chose to join him on the journey. He became part of Abraham's family and travelled with him almost as if he were his own son.

Abraham left Haran... Genesis 12:4–5. The text stresses that Lot travelled *with* Abraham.

Abraham recalled how he and Lot grew even closer when the family was forced to journey to Egypt during the famine. These were difficult times, and Lot was with him every step of the way. (Once again, Lot is described as being "with Abraham" upon their return from Egypt.) When they finally returned from their protracted Egyptian sojourn, Abraham looked forward to living in peace and prosperity with his nephew and his family.

When the family returned... Genesis 13:1.

The closeness did not last. Rich in cattle and sheep, Abraham proceeded as far as Bethel and planned on settling there. Lot, however, also had flocks and herds and tents, and the land simply could not support both families. Their possessions were so great they could not remain together.

Abraham proceeded as far... Genesis 13:2–6.

How sad, yet how similar to our own life experiences. During the difficult times in our own families, during the years when we had little and we struggled to make ends meet, there was a closeness that bonded us together. The struggle we shared helped us appreciate the importance of our brothers and sisters, our husbands and wives. Yet, often when life became easier and we became more affluent and mobile, it seemed the closeness dissipated along with the poverty or hardship. Can we forget in this regard the poignant scenes about the disintegration of the Kashinsky family in the movie Avalon, which hit so closely home? It was difficult for us to witness how this extended immigrant family, so loving and caring when they all lived in a small radius from one another in Baltimore, struggling to simply survive, fell apart when they began to succeed financially and desired the better lifestyle of the suburbs.

So, too, Abraham and Lot and their clans lived together

in harmony throughout the years of journey and famine without a hint of strife, yet later their extensive possessions indeed became a burden; one that split the family. And terrible quarreling broke about between Abraham and Lot.

The language in the text emphasizes why the family became divided. The famine was *"kaved,"* weighty, burdensome, but later they returned weighted down—*kaved* in possessions. They could survive the *ra'av*, the famine, yet because their possessions were so great *(rav)*, they could not remain together. And, indeed, strife *(riv)* erupted between them.

And terrible quarreling broke... Genesis 13:7–8.

Abraham, the champion of everyone, who always defended the downtrodden and argued for the preservation of life, could not live in peace with his own flesh and blood. The two who sojourned together from Ur to Canaan could no longer be a part of one family. Terah's family separated, with Lot travelling eastward, *mikedem* as did Adam and Eve when they left the Garden and Cain after the killing of his brother, Abel.[2] Like his predecessors, Lot left the place whence wholeness and nourishment comes, in this case his family in Canaan.

with Lot travelling... Genesis 13:9–11.

The Birth of Ishmael: Is the Bond between Father and Son Unbreakable?

Abraham thought to himself that in some ways Ishmael was just like Lot. He, too, was "the son" being sent away, and he also travelled eastward, away from Abraham's house. Not unlike our own families which have been reshaped because of divorce, in which we and our children sometimes suffer because we are forced to live far apart, Abraham was cut off from his own flesh and blood. Ishmael and Lot are also linked by the fact that the name of Ishmael's youngest son is *Kedmah,* from the same root *kedem,* meaning "east."[3]

the name of Ishmael's... Genesis 25:15.

Unlike Lot, however, Ishmael was in fact Abraham's natural son. He was not even excluded from the promise that God made to Abraham to give the land of Canaan to his offspring, to make them as numerous as the grains of sand and the stars in the sky. Now Abraham couldn't help but wonder what would become of God's promise. Would Ishmael survive the heat of the desert? Would he grow to be the father of a great nation? These questions filled his mind and heart that day when Hagar and Ishmael were banished to the desert, to a life as nomads.

Abraham also kept thinking how the years had flown by since Ishmael was born. He closed his eyes and remembered how thirteen years before, Sarah, unable to conceive, urged him to sleep with Hagar, her Egyptian handmaid, so that she could provide him with a male heir. She thought that by Hagar giving birth to a son she herself would be elevated, at least in her own eyes if not in his.[4] Sarah never imagined that he would develop any kind of special affection for Hagar's son or for that matter for the servant herself. Whatever Sarah's expectations, Abraham came to treat Hagar as a wife and have much affection for her and for his firstborn son, Ishmael. The biblical writer states very plainly that Hagar was given to him "as a wife" *(l'ishah)* and not as a concubine.[5]

For that matter, even God responded positively to Hagar and Ishmael. As Abraham recalled, when Hagar ran away from Sarah's harsh treatment after she became pregnant (while Sarah remained barren), an angel comforted her by saying that God would greatly increase her offspring, who like Sarah's progeny will be too numerous to count. The promise was clear: Ishmael would flourish like Isaac.

Furthermore, not only did God directly announce to Hagar the impending birth of a son, which never happens to Sarah, but her son's name would even bear God's name. Hagar told Abraham that God said to her: "Behold, you are with child and you shall bear a son; and you shall call him

the promise that God...
See Genesis 12:7, 13:15–17 and 15:4–5 regarding the promise.

by Hagar giving birth...
Genesis 16:2.

that God would greatly...
Genesis 16:10.

"Behold you are with...
Genesis 16:11.

Ishmael *(Yishmael)*, for the Lord has paid heed *(shama)* to your suffering." In fact, because God had spoken to her directly, Hagar, the Egyptian handmaid, is the one who called God by name: "And she called the Lord who spoke to her, "You are *El-roi* (God who sees)," by which she meant, "Have I not been able to see because [God] saw me." And because Hagar called upon God's name, the well at which God appeared to her was called *"Be'er lahai roi,"* the well of the Living One who Sees. The crucial coincidence is that this is the very place where Isaac later settles following his mother Sarah's death (Genesis 24:62).[6] The two sons of Abraham, Isaac and Ishmael, so very different, are associated with the same place, which is situated between Kadesh, the holy place, and Bered.

Hagar's relationship with the Divine and God's concern for her and for Ishmael, their son, made this moment when Abraham had to banish them from his tent even more painful. When Hagar gave birth, Abraham named the child Ishmael. It is Abraham who in the end named and indeed loved *his* son and recognized God's relationship with him.

As Abraham lingered at the entrance to his tent after Hagar and Ishmael disappeared beyond the horizon, he also remembered the day that he circumcised Ishmael. How strange that he circumcised Ishmael on the very day God revealed that he and Sarah would give birth to a son, Isaac, who would be the progenitor of a great nation. Ishmael bore the sign of the covenant on his flesh, as would Isaac. Yet, thinking that they were too old to conceive a child, Abraham responded to God's promise by pleading, "Oh that Ishmael might live by your favor!"

Although the retort surely reflected Abraham's disbelief and anxiety, it was strange that precisely at the moment when God announced Isaac's forthcoming birth, Abraham focused upon his other son about whom he was concerned and for whom he prayed.[7] But there is more here. Immediately af-

"And she called the Lord...
Genesis 16:13.

Abraham named the...
Genesis 16:15.

the day that he...
Genesis 17:16–17.

"Oh that Ishmael...
Genesis 17:18.

for whom he prayed...
Bereshit Rabbah 47:4.

ter God retorted that Sarah shall give birth to Isaac through whom the covenant will be maintained, the Divine nevertheless responds to Abraham's concerns regarding his firstborn son by emphasizing that Abraham's plea for Ishmael has been heard and he will be blessed. And the blessing? God will make him exceedingly numerous; he will be the progenitor of twelve tribes and become a great nation. Even then, Abraham was struck by how similar this promise was to that made by God concerning his other son, Isaac—both were to be fertile and numerous; to father twelve tribes; and to become a great nation. The two sons of Abraham, so different and distant from each other, will eventually possess similar blessings, even though the covenant would be established through Isaac.

the Divine nevertheless... Genesis 17:19. Note how Abraham names Isaac as he did Ishmael.

God will make him... Genesis 17:20.

Even though Isaac is the link in the chain of tradition extending from his father Abraham to his son Jacob, the tension in the biblical account between the two brothers raises questions regarding how Ishmael is to be seen and treated. It is especially poignant as a paradigm for our attitude as Jews, descendants of Isaac, toward non-Jews, in general, and our Arab brothers and sisters, in particular. In light of the present peace initiatives by Israel, its Arab neighbors and the P.L.O., it behooves us to listen to the story of Isaac and Ishmael, our progenitors.

Isaac and Ishmael:
In Our Families Children Struggle for Identity

But now Ishmael was gone and Abraham felt pangs of guilt course through him. "I never thought it would come to this," Abraham whispered to Sarah as he lay next to her that night. Summoning his courage, he added: "You know that I loved Ishmael, too, and now he's gone."

"You know that I..." The rabbis emphasize just how much Abraham cared for Ishmael. See, for example, Bereshit Rabbah 55:7.

Sarah, however, reminded Abraham that Isaac was their *ben zekunim*, the son of their old age, whom God had prom-

Sarah, however, reminded... Genesis 21:1–2.

ised to them. Isaac was her son; the one destined to be the heir to the covenant which God had sealed with Abraham many years before. Isaac was the guarantor of their future, the insurer of their immortality, and not Ishmael, who was the son of a mere Egyptian handmaid.[8] Sarah added: "Isaac was a miraculous gift from God. Though everyone laughed at the thought of me conceiving and bearing a child at the age of ninety, God brought me laughter and everyone who heard about Isaac's birth now laughed with me." The text emphasizes Isaac's importance when Sarah says: "Everyone who hears will laugh with me *(yitzhak li)*. The phrase could be read as *"Yitzhak,* Isaac, is mine!"

God brought me laughter...
Genesis 21:6.

Abraham heard his wife's words and reflected on the day and how it had started. They had invited all the members of their clan to celebrate Isaac's weaning. Isaac would surely live and grow to maturity, as God had planned. But Abraham remembered the looks on the faces of Hagar and Ishmael as they stood witnessing this great celebration. How were they to feel as "guests" at this great event knowing that no such feast took place when Ishmael grew up? Would not Ishmael have felt that he was an unimportant member of Abraham's family? Thoughts of his father not loving him must have crossed his mind that day. And Abraham could not stop thinking about his son, Ishmael, and the hurt done to him.

to celebrate Isaac's...
Genesis 21:8.

Is it any different for us? Almost every one of us, either because we are one of several children in a family or we ourselves have more than one child, knows the pain when children receive different treatment from their parents. This is especially true for those of us who live in families blended from two separate marriages. How do our stepchildren feel when they do not get the same love, attention and even privileges as those conceived by us? What goes through the minds and hearts of our own children when they see a step-brother or sister enjoy a more lavish Bar or Bat Mitzvah celebration because their other parent can afford and wants an expensive party? Each one of us knows such moments.

I have spoken to my younger brother many times about the fact that our Bar Mitzvah parties were very different. While mine took place at a somewhat lavish hotel in New York City, to which 200 guests were invited, my brother's "affair" consisted of cold cut sandwiches served to some 20 people in my parents' small apartment. Although the Bar Mitzvahs occurred some six years apart, and my father's economic situation declined over that time, it did not mollify my brother. Only years later, when we were able to talk about such experiences and confront the feelings involved, did I fully understand how my younger brother suffered because of the inequity. All of us, in one way or another, know the feelings Hagar and Ishmael must have harbored.

As Abraham thought about the day, what made matters worse was what occurred right after the weaning celebration. Sarah saw Ishmael, the son of Hagar the Egyptian, playing, *metzahhek*. At what must have been her supreme moment of happiness, the birth and weaning of this son of her old age, Sarah could only *see* one thing: Ishmael playing. Unnamed here and merely identified as the son of a slave, Ishmael is the object of her attention. What was Ishmael doing that so bothered Abraham's wife? And why at this moment, of all times, would Sarah become upset because of Ishmael? Now, at the very moment of her heightened joy at the realization that Isaac would surely live, why should what Ishmael did matter?

Sarah saw Ishmael... Genesis 21:9.

What is of course absolutely startling is the use of the term *metzahhek* which comes from the same root as the Hebrew for Isaac—*Yitzhak*, and both mean "laugh." Isaac and Ishmael, the two brothers from different mothers, nevertheless bear the same description! They are one.[9] The use of *metzahhek* as an allusion to Isaac indicates that Sarah, seeing the two brothers together, suddenly realized the close

Isaac and Ishmael... Isaac himself is described as the *metzahhek* a bit further on in the Genesis narrative (Genesis 26:8).

affinity that would develop between them and became extremely concerned about Isaac's future.[10] If they were too much alike, then Ishmael would pose a threat to Isaac's inheritance. She knew Abraham's positive feelings toward his firstborn son. Isaac's clear identity was at stake, and in Sarah's eyes Isaac could not grow up to be himself if Ishmael, his other side, was a constant presence.

Paul Berman, in a poignant article entitled "The Other and the Almost the Same," noted that the person who closely resembles us, yet who is not really our double, might end up saying: "You are almost like me. The similarity between us is so plain that in the eye of the world you are my brother. My identity consists precisely of the ways in which I am different from you. Yet the more you resemble me, the harder it is for anyone to see those crucial differences. Our resemblance threatens to obliterate everything that is special about me."[11] Sarah's fear could not be more succinctly expressed; these could be the words eventually spoken by her son Isaac to Ishmael.

From that moment on, Ishmael's fate (as well as that of his mother) was sealed: Like Cain and Lot before him, the other brother had to be sent away.

How Could Abraham Banish His Son?
Every Parent's Anguish

So Sarah directed Abraham to send Hagar and Ishmael away: "Cast out the slavewoman and her son, for the son of that slave shall not share in the inheritance with my son, Isaac." Disparagingly, Sarah does not even refer to Hagar and Ishmael by name. Sarah's angry dismissal of Abraham's "other" son is not wholly unexpected. After all, he is nothing in her eyes, and certainly not worthy of mention in the same breath as her son, and Abraham's heir, Isaac. But how should Abraham feel? How should he react to the thought

"Cast out the... Genesis 21:10.

of losing Ishmael, with whom he had built a close relationship over the past thirteen years? What is clear is the contrast between Sarah's directive and Abraham's reaction: "The matter distressed Abraham greatly because it concerned his son." Ishmael was *his* son, just as Isaac was.

Sarah may have viewed him as nothing more than a child of an Egyptian slavewoman, but Ishmael was his flesh and blood whom he loved and to lose him grieved him greatly. More than all the other misfortunes that befell Abraham in his life, the casting out of Ishmael was the most painful. In fact, Abraham is not only pictured as praying to God for Ishmael's welfare, which we would expect him to do only for Isaac, but even years later Abraham had not ceased loving his firstborn son. Abraham, in his desire to see his son, had tied a cloth around Hagar's waist dragging behind her to enable him to know the path they took. The rabbis picture Abraham as still venturing out into the wilderness to visit his son three years after Ishmael had been driven from his house. Although Sarah made him swear he would not get off the camel when visiting Hagar and Ishmael, nevertheless, he braved the desert to see the son whom he loved.

On one occasion, arriving at midday, he encountered Ishmael's wife, Ayeshah. He inquired as to where Ishmael was, and was told that he had gone to collect fruit. Abraham asked for a little bread and water because he was faint from the trek through the desert. Ayeshah responded that she had neither. He then said to her, "When Ishmael comes home, tell him that a certain old man came from the land of Canaan to see him and said to exchange the threshhold of his house for it is not good for him." When Ishmael returned, his wife related to him what had transpired and the words of the old man. Ishmael understood and divorced his wife.

Not only does this story indicate the concern and love Abraham possessed for Ishmael, but also their continuing relationship. But there is more. Abraham visits Ishmael again

"The matter distressed... Genesis 21:11.

More than all the other... Pirkei d'Rabbi Eliezer, Chapter 30.

pictured as praying to... Midrash Lekah Tov to Genesis 21:11.

The rabbis picture... Pirkei d'Rabbi Eliezer (Chapter 30) with direct parallels in Islamic oral tradition, the Hadith Literature.

sometime later and the same scene is repeated with Ishmael's second wife, Fatima. Only this time, she responds positively to Abraham's request for food, and therefore Abraham prays for his son's welfare. This results in Ishmael's household enjoying much bounty and many blessings. When Ishmael came home that day and his wife related to him what had occured, he knew that his father still loved him deeply.

Although this story concerning Abraham's relationship with Ishmael was shaped long ago in a very different world, it still rings true for us today. We divorced fathers and mothers know Abraham's pain of separation from his child. Many of us regularly journey to see our children who do not live with us and we have experienced both the anticipatory joy and exhilaration of going to see and spend time with our kids, as well as the attendant frustration and sadness of separation. We also have heard Sarah's words when she asked Abraham not to get off the camel. How terrible if Abraham were to spend intimate time with his child. And yet we and our children, like Abraham and Ishmael, not only can survive the fragmentary nature of our own relationships, but our mutual love can even grow. According to another legend, Ishmael and his entire family are pictured as journeying to Canaan to live with his father, Abraham.

According to another...
Sefer ha-Yashar, Chapter 22:1, pp. 41 a–b.

The Banishment and the Binding: Stories of Our Own Sacrifices

Abraham indeed loved both of his sons, and the love for each would be tested in the very same way: Would he be willing to sacrifice that which he loved? The banishment of Ishmael to the desert that could have meant sure death would be replayed on Mt. Moriah. Our story is about two sons of the same father who share the same fate. They are passive agents in similar dramas.

Notice how in the stories in Genesis 21 and 22, we never hear Ishmael's voice, and Isaac speaks only once. In fact, a rather startling feature of the story of the banishment of Hagar and Ishmael in Genesis 21 is the realization that Ishmael's name is not even mentioned, in contrast to Isaac who is mentioned several times. And once Isaac is born, it is almost as if the son of the maidservant, Isaac's half brother, disappears from the narrative as anonymously as he entered it. When there are two sides of a whole, only one can command center stage at a time.[12]

The parallelism and the close connection between the binding of Isaac and the banishing of Ishmael is evident from the very outset.[13] Abraham does not respond immediately to Sarah's request regarding Hagar and Ishmael, but rather to God's demand that, "Whatever Sarah tells you, do as she says." Abraham submits to the Divine call, as he does in the *Akedah* (the Binding of Isaac). Furthermore, Abraham seems to act in the same way in both stories. We are told in Genesis 21 and 22 that "Abraham rose early in the morning" in anticipation of the impending events. Zealous to do what he perceived to be God's will, or unable to sleep, or both, Abraham began his preparations as early as he could. It was his ambivalence and fright at what he was about to do that forced him out of bed early. In both cases, the father in him would not allow Abraham to linger in bed, as if a casual day's labor awaited him.

We are told in...
Genesis 21:14
and 22:3.

Therefore, having received God's guarantees about both Isaac's and Ishmael's future, Abraham gave Hagar provisions for the road and, placing Ishmael on her shoulder as he would later place the wood for the sacrifice on Isaac's shoulder, he sent her away. Had he given her enough food and water to reach an oasis, or was he an accomplice to the murder of both the maidservant and her son? Whatever would be the outcome, it seemed that it was Hagar who alone would shoulder the burden of her son.

Abraham gave Hagar...
Genesis 21:14
and 22:6.

Even more difficult for us than the question of how Abraham felt, is how Hagar and Ishmael felt. Driven from the only home they had known and now disoriented and wandering in the desert, what might they have thought about Abraham, whom they always believed had cared for them? Displaced from their home with their future in doubt, fearing that they might not survive the heat and the aridity of the desert, how could they feel anything but a deep animosity for Abraham, the patriarch of the nation of Israel. They were not unlike their descendants, today's Ishmaelites, who feel that they, too, have been driven from their homes by the heirs to Abraham's covenant. To be sure, history teaches that many Palestinians voluntarily abandoned their homes at the outbreak of Israel's War of Independence at the behest of the leaders of the Arab world who guaranteed them that in a matter of days they would drive the Jews into the sea. Then every Arab who had left his ancestral home would return to the land of their fathers and mothers and inherit the possessions of their former Jewish neighbors. Although this view of the history of the Middle East is correct, it is not what today's descendants of Ishmael believe. The refugees who live in the camps in Gaza and the West Bank, not far from where Abraham dwelt with Sarah and Isaac, can only feel that their land and homes have been taken from them and they have been driven unjustly into the wilderness, there to struggle for survival like Hagar and Ishmael with little hope for the future.

And when the water skin was depleted, Hagar began to panic, fearing the worst—the death of her son. And feeling absolutely helpless, she cast the child away from her since she could not bear watching him die. She placed Ishmael under a bush and moved far from him, raised her voice and burst into tears. The text says, "she raised her voice and cried," just as Abraham "raised his eyes" in order to see the mountain from afar—God's place, the place of deliverance,

she cast the child...
Genesis 21:15–16.

[76]

in the story of the *Akedah.* Hagar was resigned to the fact that both she and her son were about to die, as they were surely not anywhere near a watering hole. But God could not abandon the boy, who like Isaac had to fulfill his destiny to become a great nation. And even though it was Hagar who had cried out in despair, God heard the voice of Ishmael—*yishma El* (God heard), as the Divine hears the voices of all humanity, and immediately responded to the plight of Abraham's firstborn son. Twice we are told that "God heard the cry of the boy." We cannot help but understand that God's focus is upon the lad, *na'ar* in Hebrew, and in the guise of an angel comes to save his life by calling out from heaven. Again, the climax of the story is so reminiscent of the *Akedah.* At the denouement of the story in Genesis 22, we read that "Abraham *cast forth his hand* to pick up the knife to slay his son. Then an angel of the Lord called to him from heaven: "Abraham! Abraham!" And he answered: "Here I am." And [the angel] said: "Do not *cast your hand* upon the boy or do anything to him." An angel's voice called from heaven at the critical moment to insure that this boy, this *na'ar,* Isaac, would be saved. As Hagar had cast forth Ishmael, so Abraham cast forth his hand to slay his son, but God was with the lad, for he, too, was destined for blessing.

Similarly, an angel (a *malach*) of God called to Hagar, saying, "*Mahlach* Hagar," what troubles you, Hagar, thus calming her fears. It was as if the sound play in the text was teaching us that God indeed had sent Hagar her own angel (*malach* Hagar), telling her that the Divine had heard the cry of the child. God understood his plight and would show his mother that she possessed the strength to save him. It was not enough for Hagar to raise (*tissa*) her voice in anguish; now she had to raise up (*se'i*) the child.

Although God responded to the cries, she was told that she herself would have to grab hold of her son. God says to

in the story...
Genesis 22:4.

destiny to become...
Genesis 21:17–18.

"Abraham cast forth...
Genesis 22:10–12.

God says to her...
Genesis 21:18.

[77]

her, *"Hahaziki et yadeich bo,"* hold him by the hand. Yet, if translated literally, the words mean "strengthen your hand on or through him." It is as if the angel/God is saying: "If you simply raise him up and hold him, you yourself will be made strong." The beginning of Hagar's own salvation was her ability to reach out to Ishmael and give him the support he needed to survive. God had opened her eyes to her own strength and she immediately saw a well that would save them. Listen to the the words in Hebrew: *"Va-yifkakh Elohim et eiyneha,* God opened her eyes *(eineha)."* However, *ayin,* in addition to meaning "eye," can also mean "well." Once she had reached out to hold Ishmael, the wellsprings of her own being were opened, which then enabled her to see the well nearby. Though the well, the source of their redemption, was there the entire time she was sitting a distance away from Ishmael, only now was she able to truly know that it existed. And she went and she filled the water skin, and proceeded to give her son drink. God was truly with Ishmael (not only with Isaac), and as a result Ishmael would live.

"Va-yifkakh Elohim... Genesis 21:19.

And she went and... Genesis 21:20.

Like Ishmael's mother, his contemporary descendants are learning that they have the ability to insure their own survival and must take responsibility for it. They, too, can shape a positive future for their children, if only they can see that the desert can flourish like an oasis. And they are not alone. They are not only Abraham's children, but also God's children, and as such the power in the universe which makes for wholeness is as much a part of them as it is with their Israeli brothers and sisters. Though we Jews believe in our unique role as descendants of Isaac and his son Jacob, we recognize that God hears the cries of all peoples and responds accordingly.

But the lesson to be learned is not only meant for today's descendants of Ishmael. All of us are like Hagar, the Egyptian handmaid who bore Abraham's first son. Each one of us has to be able to recognize the well of water in our midst, in us—the power that we ourselves possess to make our own lives better. But ironically, it is only when we reach out to others, especially to those whom we love—our spouses, children, parents, lovers, and friends, that we come in touch with the depth of our own strength. Perhaps, in the end, that precisely is *our* test. Lost in the deserts of our own lives, searching desperately for a way to survive the difficult journey with those whom we love, we can come to know our essential natures through the degree to which we can touch others. The angel told Hagar, *"hahaziki et yadeich bo,"* strengthen your hands on/through him, and at that moment, each one of us was challenged to reach out to our loved ones and in so doing gain uplift ourselves.

Our Final Test:
Acting When There Are No Guarantees
that We Will Succeed

Ishmael survived due to God's response to his cries and his mother's reaching out to him. Abraham had cast out his son, assured that he would survive the desert journey because of God's words of comfort and pledge that he would make of Ishmael's progeny a great nation. All that he had provided for Ishmael's and Hagar's sustenance was some bread and a lone skin of water. However, these meager provisions would surely enable them to reach an oasis before giving out under the heat of the desert sun since God had guaranteed the boy's future. Ishmael, whom he loved dearly, would prosper under God's watchful eye, as he himself had prospered these many years. Yahweh had always been there for him; from the arduous trek from Haran to the land of Canaan, the famine and the exhausting trip to Egypt, the battle against powerful enemies in Canaan as well as his own family turmoil. Now God would protect his son Ishmael.

God's words of comfort...
Genesis 21:12–13.

Ishmael would become the...
Genesis 17:20.

Ishmael would become the father of a great nation made up of twelve powerful tribes, just as his half-brother Isaac.[14]

In some way, perhaps, the guarantee regarding Ishmael explains why precisely at this moment the need for one final test of Abraham became apparent. One more trial was needed, since God had to know if Abraham was willing to put his son's (in this case Isaac's) life on the line when there was no explicit guarantee given that he would be spared.

God told him was...
Genesis 22:2.

All that God told him was that he should take Isaac to the land of Moriah and offer him there on one of the mountains which God would show him. On the contrary, it would have seemed to Abraham that God's previous promise of making his progeny as numerous as the stars in the sky, which was to be fulfilled through Isaac, was now doomed. In sacrificing Isaac, he was giving up his own future and immortality. At Moriah, God would know just how deep Abraham's faith was and just how far he would go in giving up his own ego needs.

"It came to pass...
Genesis 22:1.

And so "it came to pass after these things that God put Abraham to the test." Although the phrase, "And it came to pass after these things," is clearly formulaic and should be translated as "sometime later," yet we would immediately ask: What event(s) preceded the *Akedah* which gave rise to it? What "things" occurred which made it necessary for God to demand that Abraham sacrifice his son Isaac?

The rabbis believed...
Bereshit Rabbah 55:4.

The rabbis believed that the juxtaposition of events implied a causal relationship between them. Therefore, the *Akedah,* which followed upon Isaac's birth and weaning, and Ishmael's banishment, must have occurred because of one or both of these events. Perhaps, as they argue, the sacrifice of Isaac was necessary because of Abraham's misgivings about the depth of his faith. Having just celebrated the birth and weaning of Isaac with a gala feast, Abraham is pictured as feeling unworthy of this gift and unappreciative of God's benevolence. Accordingly, it was because of these feelings that the Divine had to test Abraham. Both God and Abraham had to know if he could sacrifice the object of his greatest love, the child who would bear his legacy, Isaac. The rabbis are right. Although Abraham had succeeded in passing every test that God had placed upon him, including the banishment of Hagar and Ishmael, in each case God had guaranteed the outcome in one way or another. But could Abraham sacrifice Isaac, the very guarantor of the future? Would Abraham be willing to sacrifice the promised greatness for his progeny, in essence his own immortality, all of which depended upon Isaac's survival?

Hineini: *Responding to the Other—* ### *As Humans We Are Challenged to Be Present*

In God's desire to see if he, like each of us in our own way, can survive in a world which lacks guarantees, the Divine called to Abraham from the heavens. Upon hearing God's call, Abraham responded with the word *hineini*, affirming his willingness to do whatever God would ask of him.[15] Abraham did not wait for God to spell out the task nor did he ask for any guarantees. This is exactly what the term *hineini* signifies—being ready to respond within the context of relationship, regardless of the nature of the request. *Hineini* can teach us about the very essence of relationship; about our relationships, not only with God but with other human beings.

God's call... Genesis 22:1.

Abraham himself uses the term *hineini* to respond to Isaac's petition as they begin to ascend the mountain, after travelling for three days. Abraham responds to his son as he responded to God—*hineini*, here I am for you. When we respond to those we love, our parents, spouses, or our children, it is tantamount to responding to the highest call. And it really does not matter what the request is to which we must respond. In Abraham's case, there is little he can do

Abraham responds to... Genesis 22:7.

for Isaac, other than simply reassuring him through his presence. Perhaps that is all he really needed.

So it is with each of us. For many years prior to his death, my father suffered as a stroke victim who was more or less confined to the house. Pop was dependent on members of the family to care for his daily needs, including shopping. It was a common occurrence during the week for him to call me in my office and ask: "Normyboy (I always knew he wanted something when he called me "Normyboy!"), do me a favor on your way home, please stop over and go to the grocery store and buy me some milk, bread." However, early on, when I arrived at his apartment and looked into the refrigerator, I would be astonished to find that the very items that Pop had requested were sitting on the shelf. Eventually, I got the point—it wasn't a matter of what he requested; what mattered was my readiness to do for him. All he wanted was for his son to respond, *"hineini"*—Here I am Pop; I love you. I had to learn the meaning of *hineini*.

In Abraham's case, God or perhaps Abraham himself needed to know if he was ready to respond to God without any sense of what was being asked of him and without any guarantee that it would go well for him and his family. The difficulty and the suspense of the test is clearly emphasized in the possible conversation which took place due to God's vague instructions to Abraham. Just listen to the imagined dialogue: "And [God] said: 'Take your son.' 'Which son?' Abraham asked. 'Your only son,' God replied. 'But each is the only son of his mother,' was Abraham's response. God added: 'Whom you love.' 'Is there a limit to the affections?' asked Abraham. And God finally said: 'Isaac.'"

"And [God] said... Bereshit Rabbah 55:7.

This interchange shows how the importance of the test is enhanced by the degree of uncertainty implicit in God's words. It is not clear to Abraham which son is the object of God's command. And for that matter, he loves both of them; there is no distinction here between Ishmael and Isaac.

[82]

Furthermore, the measure of ambiguity and uncertainty is extended in God's ensuing instructions: "Go to the land of Moriah and offer him there as a burnt offering on one of the mountains which I will point out to you." The fact that God does not reveal to Abraham his ultimate destination underscores God's desire to see whether he can act without having any certainty as to where he is going and what the outcome of the journey will be. Perhaps certainty and direction can only come once he has dared to begin the journey!

"Go to the Land... Genesis 22:2.

Abraham's Eagerness to Prove His Fidelity: Self-involvement Makes Us Oblivious to the Ones We Love

Abraham seemingly could not wait to fulfill God's command. He needed to demonstrate to God (or perhaps to himself) that he could fulfill any command, even if no guarantees were given. Therefore, he got up at the crack of dawn and prepared for the journey by himself, not allowing his servants to participate. Abraham's zealous behavior and intensity is furthur evident when he and Isaac arrive at the sacrificial site. Abraham does all the work himself; building an altar there, laying out the wood and binding his son Isaac.

he got up at... Genesis 22:3.

building an altar... Genesis 22:9.

Abraham is so self-involved that he acts like an automaton; all his actions are staccato as he prepares for the sacrifice in a very methodical fashion. There is no sign of any emotion on Abraham's part though he is about to take his son's life. All that we see is Abraham, the knight of faith, whose mission it was to fulfill what he perceived to be God's wish; Abraham the father, who was given a gift of life in his old age, is not to be found on the mountaintop.

And as Abraham raised the knife to slay his son, an angel called to him from heaven: "Abraham," as God had called out his name at the outset of the test. But this time, Abraham did not not respond immediately. So consumed by the task

an angel called... Genesis 22:11.

at hand and so altogether bent upon demonstrating his unconditional fidelity, he was oblivious to the angel's call. And so the angel boomed forth one more time: "Abraham!" At that moment, Abraham, the father, was finally awakened to the reality of what he was about to do, and he responded as before, *"hineini"*—here I am.

We are all like Abraham; each of us is so involved in our outside worlds—our careers, interests, or our principles—that we do not or cannot see that it is our child, or spouse or parent that is bound on the altar. We are so adept at sacrificing that which is truly important to us on the altars we have erected that we may ask whether we are capable of hearing the cry of the angel before it is too late. And those of us who are blessed to be rabbis, cantors, educators and communal workers are no exception; in some ways, perhaps we are the most vulnerable in this regard. We who see ourselves as doing "God's work" when we are constantly there for others, when we spend so many hours of our day responding to our congregants and the members of the wider community, must begin to understand Abraham as he walks with his son on the road to the mountain. For when

Isaac calls out...
Genesis 22:7.

Isaac calls out to Abraham, "My father," saying to him, "As you walk on this journey of such universal import, when all is said and done, where are you for me? Am I important in your life?" he calls out to each one of us. It is my son who is speaking to me and saying, "I know that you're busy dad, but do you have some time to watch the basketball game with me tonight?" and it is so easy to blurt out, "Ilan, I'm tired. Some other time." At those very moments, would that we would have the strength to respond *"hineini,"* in the fullness of its meaning; would that I could say more often, "Sure, Ilan, nothing could give me more pleasure!"

This then was the final part of Abraham's test: Would he have the strength to heed the call of the angel/his son as he had responded to God's call at the outset of the drama?

Would Abraham now be able to sacrifice his own needs and truly listen to the voice of the Divine (as conveyed by the angel/Isaac)? As Abraham had to sacrifice his own feelings towards Ishmael when God asked him to respond to Sarah's demand that he banish Hagar and Ishmael, so, too, here at the climax of the *Akedah,* Abraham had to transcend his own ego in order to insure that Isaac would live. Could he see beyond himself and recognize his real source of strength; that which would insure his own future?

Opening One's Eyes to the Source of Redemption: If Only We Could Discern God's Presence

But Abraham was so bent on proving himself that he was oblivious when the angel called out from the heavens in an attempt to prevent him from taking his son's life. He did not hear a thing. At that moment, God implored the archangel Michael, saying: "Why are you standing there? He's about to kill the boy! Don't allow him to be slaughtered." Although Michael argued with God, saying that he did not have the strength to stop Abraham, God pushed him out of the heavens and Michael cried out: "Abraham, lay not your hand upon the boy, neither do anything to him!" Abraham responded, "God commanded me to slaughter Isaac and you command me not to slaughter him. The words of the teacher and the words of the disciple—to whose words should I harken?" So it was that God was forced to intervene and called out to Abraham, "By Myself have I sworn....because you have done this thing and have not withheld your son."

In the end, Abraham indeed harkened to the Divine voice as it implored him not to take Isaac's life. And redemption came in the form of a ram which was caught by its horns in a thicket. According to the legend, the ram sacrificed in Isaac's stead was one of the redemptive vehicles created at

he was oblivious... Genesis 22:11.

At that moment... Genesis 22:16. This is a reworking of a tradition found in *Midrash Va-Yosha.*

in the form of a... Genesis 22:13.

According to the legend... Pirkei d'Rabbi Eliezer, Chapter 31.

the twilight of the sixth day of Creation, prior to the first Shabbat.[16] Programmed in from the very beginning of human existence, it was as if the ram was situated on the mountain top from the beginning of time, patiently waiting for the propitious moment. But had Abraham not raised his eyes and caught a glimpse of the ram entangled in the brush, the redemptive animal could never have fulfilled the role it was destined to play. Yet, even though he saw the ram in the thicket, Abraham did not make a move toward the animal. He was frozen on the spot. But the ram made sure that Abraham would see it. Situated behind him, the ram put forth its leg and grabbed the corner of Abraham's coat.[17] Abraham then turned around, saw the animal, and rushed to take it and offer it in place of his son, Isaac. The vehicles for holiness and redemption are not only ever-present, waiting for us to open our hearts, minds and eyes to them, but they constantly beckon us to reach out and take hold of them. As resistent as we are to doing good and improving our relationships and our lives, the Divine in the world echoes around us and within us, demanding that we respond and fulfill our highest selves.

The Aftermath of the Akedah: Facing Our Own Isolation

Yet, the near sacrifice of Isaac surely must have taken a tremendous toll on him, as well as on his father. If only Isaac could speak to us, we would hear the pain and the hurt that he must have felt being placed upon the altar of his father's beliefs and ego needs that fateful day on the top of Mt. Moriah. But it isn't difficult to recreate Isaac's feelings and anguish. You can just imagine what he would say:

"The road to the top of the mountain was rugged and we climbed with considerable difficulty. When we reached the top, I unloaded the kindling wood which father had put on my back, and he took the firebrand and the slaughtering knife. 'But where is the lamb for the offering?' I asked in wonderment. My father remained silent for a moment, then he said: 'Adonai will select the lamb for the offering.' 'Adonai? I don't understand. What does Adonai have to do with this?' And then my father said: 'My son....' It was painful for him to say that. His voice seemed to break. And then I finally understood. No....I don't think I really understood. But this much I know. My father seized me and brought me to the heap of wood. He bound my hands and feet tightly. My eyes stared wide, desparately wide; his eyes were glassy and without expression. I wanted to stammer: 'Adonai.' I tried to whisper 'Adonai.' 'Adonai?' I asked. And my father unsheathed the knife, and it drew closer and closer and closer. 'Adonai!!' I cried out inaudibly, 'Adonai, Lord of the universe, where are you?' And my father placed the blade to my throat....'What are you doing?' 'Are you crazy?' 'I do not want to die....Why are you doing this?....Let me go!!....Let me go, I tell you!'

Father is now dead, and his death does not pain me in the least. On the contrary, I am almost glad that it happened. I feel like singing aloud; making an end of this mockery; tearing off the mask of mourning....Do you know that ever since that day I never spoke another word to my father. There was only silence between us. I hated my father! I always see him standing there with the knife in his hand...ready to kill me."[18]

The rupture of the relationship between Abraham and Isaac as a result of Abraham's intention to sacrifice his son on the altar he created is hinted at when Abraham descends from the mountain. Abraham returned to his [two] servants, who were waiting at the foot of the mountain, and they departed together for Be'er Sheva. When Abraham descended from Mount Moriah, he was conspicuously alone. The fact that the two servants returned *together (yachdav)* with Abraham to Be'er Sheva emphatically underscores Isaac's

Abraham returned to his...
Genesis 22:19.

absence.[19] All Abraham had were his two servants. He would never see Isaac again!

Abraham, the patriarch, the head of the Israelite clan, was indeed alone. Isaac and Ishmael, victims of their father's beliefs, were gone. Abraham was bereft of his children.[20] In addition, Hagar had been banished and he also would never see Sarah again. When Abraham returned to Be'er Sheva from Moriah, his wife was not there. As the story unfolds, Sarah was in Kiryat Arba, where she died and Abraham is pictured as travelling to Be'er Sheva to mourn for his wife.[21]

Sarah was in Kiryat...
Genesis 23:1–2.

The picture of Abraham at this juncture is surely a disturbingly sad one: The tribal patriarch, leader of his clan, who has lost those closest and most dear to him. But we ask, "Is it too late for Abraham? Is this what he has to look forward to—a life of isolation, cut off from his own progeny and the promise of the future?" And as we frame the question, dare we ask it of ourselves as well? Is it too late for us, we who also are so adept at sacrificing on the altars which we have erected—the altars of our careers, interests, hobbies—the ones whom we love so dearly? Are we oblivious to the cry of the angel until it is too late!

The First Steps towards Integration:
Is Rapprochement Possible within Our Families?

Is it too late for Abraham, the husband and father? In one sense it is, since he never sees his wives and children again. But perhaps not. Perhaps at the climactic moment, when the angel called out a second time, Abraham was awakened to the reality that it was his *ben zekunim,* the son of his old age, whom he was ready to kill. And that he indeed had been willing to sacrifice both his beloved sons. Hearing the piercing heavenly cry, "Abraham, Abraham"—Abraham, the father of Isaac, and Abraham, the father of Ishmael, recognized himself for the first time and left the mountain a changed person.

The change in Abraham is evident in the great emotion he exhibits upon Sarah's death. Abraham came to Kiryat Arba to mourn for her, and perhaps for the very first time in his life he sheds tears for someone for whom he cares. The text here seems to be redundant. It says that "[he] came to mourn for Sarah and cry for her" (Genesis 23:2). One would presume that his mourning for his wife would involve his crying. However, the writer goes out of the way to indicate that Abraham not only went through the formal ritual of mourning, but he indeed was deeply affected by her death. His crying for her is emphasized by the fact that the word *livkotah,* to cry for her, is written with a small *kaf.* Abraham cried over the death of his wife, emoting as he had never done before. And why did he grieve exceedingly for her? Perhaps out of guilt over his failure during her lifetime or maybe because he came to realize how much she meant to him after all. And the irony is that Abraham and Sarah came together in death as they never seemed to be in life. They were buried next to each other in the Cave of Machpelah, in the field of Efron the Hittite, which was located in Kiryat Arba.

Abraham cried over the death... B.T. *Mo'ed Katan* 27b.

But there is much more! In the following chapter, the same Abraham who would have taken his son's life had the angel not intervened goes to great lengths to find the right wife for Isaac. He sends his servant, Eliezer, on the arduous journey back to Aram Naharayim and will spare no expense to insure that Isaac marry a woman from his tribe.

And most surprisingly, when Eliezer returns with Rebekkah, Isaac is pictured as coming from the Negev, from the place named *Be'er lahai roi,* where he seems to have spent much time.[22] How meaningful that Isaac settles in the place to which Hagar fled when Sarah mistreated her prior to giving birth to Ishmael.[23] Could it possibly be that Isaac and Ishmael actually might have seen each other again,

Isaac is pictured as... Genesis 24:62.

the place to which... Genesis 16:14.

following Sarah's death?[24]

And perhaps both Isaac and Ishmael did even see their father Abraham again somewhat later. For it is told in another legend that the woman Abraham married towards the end of his life, named Keturah, was in fact Hagar. Remarrying Hagar, Abraham began to reconstitute his relationship with his son Ishmael as well.

told in another legend...
Genesis 25:1. See Bereshit Rabbah 61:4, Tanhuma Buber, *Chayei Sarah* 9 and Pirkei d'Rabbi Eliezer, Chapter 30.

both Isaac and Ishmael...
Genesis 25:9.

And even if Isaac and Ishmael did not meet before, it is not surprising that when Abraham dies, both Isaac and Ishmael come to the Cave of Machpelah to bury their father. It does not take much imagination to picture the scene as it might have unfolded that day in the field of Ephron, the Hittite, facing Mamre. Isaac stood near the cave, gazing toward the southwest from where Ishmael would come. In the distance, he could see the dust clouds indicating that a caravan was approaching. He knew that this had to be Ishmael, and he began to tremble ever so slightly. Would he recognize his half brother after all these years? Surely time will have taken its toll. And will Ishmael harbor a grudge against him because of all that happened over a score of years before? What do brothers say to each other to fill the chasm of time, distance and life experiences? Two estranged brothers, so dissimilar, yet who share the pain and anguish of life-threatening trials only to be saved by the hand of the angel, now face each other. Two brothers who knew the trauma of being a son of Abraham, finally come together and we wonder what they can possible say to one another at that moment. Suddenly the camels were close by. Isaac saw Ishmael get down and, looking up, he caught sight of his brother and their eyes met. And then Isaac saw a smile on Ishmael's face and they moved quickly towards each other. The years vanished as they embraced, kissed one another, and cried together.

Can brothers or sisters come together after years of separation, and realize how much time has been lost and how they still love each other? Every family knows this moment of meeting—the moment when siblings look into each other's eyes and search for words after years of being apart. I can remember as if it were yesterday a moment over forty years ago when I saw my father and his brother (my uncle) Moe embracing in the living room of our apartment and crying in each other's arms after not speaking to each other for many years. Having gone into business together, they experienced a falling out and not only did the two divide up the business, but they went their separate ways. And then one day, they faced each other, wondering how they could have allowed the time to slip away, and they searched for words of consolation. And we ourselves, who perhaps have not spoken to one of our brothers or sisters for a long time and wonder if we ever will, know the pain and yet the potential joy of seeing our sibling again.

Can Isaac and Ishmael come together and live in peace with one another? Can the wounds of the past be healed as the memories of struggle for position and power fade? Can the children of Abraham embrace as they stand in the fields near Hevron? Even with the real concerns of Isaac and Ishmael, as with their descendants, for their own survival and continuity, perhaps it isn't merely a dream to envision the family unified again after so many years of strife. After all, they were brothers who never lost a sense that they were the sons of the same father, who both loved them and caused them each so much pain. And perhaps they knew deep in their hearts that one day they would meet and embrace.[25]

A Newfound Harmony—yet There Are Distinctions: Will the Struggle Ever End for Us?

But is there full harmony between them? Have the two parts of Abraham's life come together totally? Even now, as the two sons stand together at the Cave of Machpelah, it is Isaac

Abraham willed all...
Genesis 25:5–6.

he in effect was...
See Bereshit Rabbah 57:3 and B.T. *Baba Batra* 16b.

God seals the fate...
Genesis 25:11.

The text goes out...
Genesis 25:12, 19.

who is seen as the preferred son who deserves to inherit his father's possessions and the blessing for the future. Prior to his death, Abraham willed all that he owned to Isaac. And he sent all of his other progeny away from his son Isaac. Though not Abraham's firstborn, Isaac was the heir to Abraham's wealth and position; he in effect was given the birthright, while Ishmael and the other siblings were banished from the family. They were sent eastward, to the place called *Kedem,* as were Adam and Eve, Cain and Lot before them. Abraham himself had not gone so far as to actually bless Isaac, while withholding such a blessing from Ishmael, feeling that such a final act would certainly undo the harmony that had been achieved. However, God seals the fate of Abraham's sons by blessing Isaac after Abraham's death.

Isaac and Ishmael had come together at the end of Abraham's life; but after he died, the bond was again broken. The distinction between them is underscored by the genealogies which follow. For all that Ishmael and Isaac are similar, in that they both give rise to twelve flourishing tribes, the text goes out of its way to describe Ishmael as "Abraham's son, whom Hagar the Egyptian, Sarah's slave, bore to Abraham," while stressing that Isaac was "the son of Abraham; Abraham begot Isaac" immediately afterwards.

Ishmael, the son of the bondwoman, was not equal to Isaac, who was to be Abraham's heir, and never would be.

The two sides, Isaac and Ishmael—brothers, antagonists—were joined, but only momentarily. Their meeting and embrace affirm the possibility that integration and unity is achievable, though in their own lives and in the lives of their descendants the struggle continues. Return to the garden remains a dream.

| | | |

CHAPTER FOUR

JACOB AND ESAU

Twins Struggle for Identity

From the moment of their conception, Jacob and Esau were engaged in a bitter struggle for survival. Though twins, two halves of a whole, they were very different and were forced to separate as they could not live in close proximity. The tension between them, exacerbated by their parents' affections and interests, led to open conflict, though they never stopped needing what the other possessed.

When we confront the tensions between Jacob and Esau, and their different relationships with their parents, we cannot help but reflect upon our brothers and sisters, and the way we interacted with our parents as we were growing up. We know Esau's pain when his brother usurps his blessing, just as we can relate to Jacob's fear as he anticipates his reunion with Esau twenty years later.

The story forces us to wonder whether we, like the two children of Isaac and Rebekkah, can overcome the differences we have experienced with our own siblings and move closer together? Through our own struggles with the angel, the shadows of ourselves, our other sides, can we move to a greater sense of wholeness and peace? Will we ever be able to embrace our brother or sister again? Can we ever live together in harmony with our brother or sister?

Jacob sat on his camel for a long time watching as Esau and his entourage of four hundred men slowly made their way southeastward toward the mountains of Seir. How naive Esau was to believe that the two of them and their families could dwell together after so much had happened. Although he told Esau that they would eventually catch up to him in Seir, Jacob had no intention of ever living with his brother in the same place. Yes, they had found a way to make peace with one another after all the strife and bitterness twenty years before, but Jacob knew that their basic differences would not allow them to live together in the same place. He thought of the stories he was told about how the two of them fought even in their mother's womb and how this was a sign that they were destined to live separate lives. So, as he watched Esau's caravan disappear over the far away hills, he motioned to his family to follow him as he turned west toward Shechem.

Although he told Esau...
Genesis 33:16–17.

The Struggle Commences at Conception:
Is Tension Inevitable among Siblings?

From the very outset of her pregnancy, Rebekkah experienced a great deal of pain as her two sons struggled in the womb. It was so bad that at times her insides felt as if they were being ripped apart by the fighting and all she could do was to cry out in her suffering, "If I must bear such pain, what good is life?"[1] It seemed to Rebekkah that Jacob and Esau were literally tearing each other apart prior to being born. From the moment of conception, tension and enmity existed between them.[2]

"If I must...
Genesis 25:22.

And when siblings fight, it causes heartache for their parents. We who are blessed to be parents can surely attest to the pain we feel when there is conflict among our own children; and we as children can remember how we hurt our parents, as well. I can vividly recall a conversation I had with my father some ten years ago prior to his death, following a squabble that occurred between my brother and me. My brother and I came to a misunderstanding that we needed to work through. That argument caused Pop a great deal of pain. In no way could he tolerate the two of us being at odds or mistreating each other, and insisted that I as the older sibling had to do something about it. The pain was written all over his face and affected him deeply. When we brothers fought he was torn part. And so we can sense the anguish Rebekkah experienced as her children struggled inside her.

Yet, whether she liked the message or not, Rebekkah is told by an oracle that she will give birth to twins who in years to come will give rise to two nations at odds with each other.[3] One nation shall be stronger than the other, and the elder shall serve the younger. The word the oracle emphasized was *yipparedu,* meaning "[they] shall be separated," which clearly alarmed Rebekkah.[4] The oracle seemed to say that her sons would always be in conflict. As similar as these twins might be, they could never live together. They indeed were twins—two halves of one whole, close and bonded together.[5] But Jacob and Esau, the two sides, had to separate because they were so different.

One nation shall...
Genesis 25:23.

The myrtle and thornbush grow side by side, and in their early stages seem identical. Yet, when they attain maturity, one is known for its fragrance, the other for its thorns. Similarly, Jacob and Esau could not have been more dissimilar, as their mother noticed the minute they burst forth from her womb. Esau was quite dark, almost reddish in complexion, and had a great deal of hair, while Jacob was fairer and smooth-skinned. These different descriptions may bear traces of the classic distinction between two types of individuals—the civilized human being and the wild, hairy hunter.[6] The contrast is underscored further by the fact that Esau later becomes an outdoorsman who hunts, while Jacob

The myrtle and thornbush...
Bereshit Rabbah 63:10 and Midrash Tanhuma ha-Nidpas, *Ki Teze* 4.

Esau was dark...
Genesis 25:25 and 27:11.

is the exact opposite. He is a mild-mannered type who prefers to remain at home. When Isaac and Rebekkah came to naming their sons, the impressions the twins made at birth led to the choice of names. They called their firstborn child *Eisav*, because his large size, ruddy color and hairy arms and legs reminded them of the constellation of stars known as the Great Bear, the *Ash*. And since Esau came out of the womb very quickly, the name *Eisav* fit because the root *ash* also means "to hurry." In contrast, Jacob was born second and Rebekkah noticed that Jacob's right hand seemed to be holding Esau's foot. They therefore called him *Ya'akov*, because he held on to his brother's heel, his *akev*. It almost seemed that Jacob was trying to prevent Esau from being born; as if he were holding him back. The name *Ya'akov* also comes from the Hebrew root *akav* which means "to delay" or "to restrain." Their names tell us that Esau would be a person of action, impulsive and quick to respond, while his brother would be slower, more calculating and thoughtful.

At first glance, the names chosen by Isaac and Rebekkah seem to fit quite well. Esau is the shrewd one, cunning and "streetwise," as he would have to be to survive as a hunter. Jacob is the tentdweller, sheltered and innocent. He is *tam*, mild, plain, or even naive. Yet, *tam* also means upright or perfect. He would surely possess moral integrity. But is this an apt description of Jacob, *Ya'akov*, the heel, the deceitful one, who is about to steal his brother's birthright?[7] The ambiguous term *tam* surely helps us as readers anticipate the coming events. But there is more. The name forces us to think about Jacob's moral stature and consider the essential natures of both brothers.[8] In so doing, we are confronted with our own characters and personalities—the Esau and Jacob in each of us.

The Objects of Their Parents' Affections:
The Beginning of Conflict with Our Siblings

The contrast and tension between the two brothers is heightened by the fact that each was the favorite of a different parent. Isaac loved Esau because he had a taste for the game Esau hunted. But Rebekkah loved Jacob, who spent hours with her in the tent. The strife that developed between the two brothers might have been fostered in part by the biased affections of their parents.

Isaac loved Esau...
Genesis 25:28.

Even today we parents sometimes inflame the relationships among our children by the way we treat them and show our affection. Even when we try to be even-handed, children sometimes feel we are not as close to them as we are to a brother or sister, and then, who better to take out their frustrations on than the object of their jealousy? How many times have we heard one of our kids say, "How come So- and-So gets to go and I cannot?" Or "Why is it that you never yell at my sister and only pick on me?"

In any event, it is not surprising that Rebekkah was closer to Jacob, as they shared so much time together. She loved telling him stories of the family's past. Yet, we wonder why Isaac was drawn to his firstborn, Esau. It would seem that father and son had absolutely nothing in common; they were completely opposite. Isaac was somewhat passive, mild and sickly, while Esau was an active, virile sportsman. What was it that caused Isaac to love Esau, whom we know responded to his father's affection?

Isaac, grown old, was dependent upon Esau to provide him with his food. It was Esau, the skillful hunter who each day brought home the tasty meat his father loved.[9] Is this so different from our own families in which an aging parent is dependent upon one child, usually by virtue of geographic proximity, for his or her care and sustenance? We know what happens in these cases: How a father or mother comes to

It was Esau...
Genesis 25:27.

depend upon one child in particular, and how this affects the other siblings. In our family, my brother always lived far away from New York. For many years he resided in Israel and raised his family there. As a result, during my father's protracted illness I took care of most of his needs. This situation, so typical of families today, in which siblings and relatives live far apart, was difficult for all of us. The attendant guilt and frustration, at times unspoken, was always there. It did not matter how much my brother loved Pop; he simply wasn't in a position to do more. Isaac had a taste for the game Esau was able to provide. The result was that father and son became bonded in a special way.

Perhaps what he needed from Esau was something else. Isaac probably was attracted to his son because of the qualities he himself did not possess.[10] Isaac loved Esau precisely because he craved what Esau could provide; even what Esau was as a person. Perhaps Isaac longed to be different. Even we, as parents, are often drawn to the child most unlike us, as if we find in him or her the missing part of ourselves; as if through that child we achieve a greater wholeness.

Esau also must have reminded Isaac of his long lost sibling, Ishmael, who was a hunter, a man of the field, wild and impetuous. Drawing close to Esau enabled Isaac to overcome in part the guilt and the loneliness he must have felt after Ishmael was banished from his father's household. Esau also enabled him to recreate his relationship with Ishmael, his other side. Even to be like him. The bond between father and son somehow must have filled the void his brother's leaving created in Isaac's life.[11]

Ishmael, who was a hunter...
Genesis 16:12 and 21:20.

Giving Up the Birthright:
Are We Jealous of What Our Brother or Sister Possesses?

The contrast between Jacob and Esau could not be more evident than in the story of the theft of the birthright. The narrative is terse, but the brothers' interaction is poignant. Just listen. Once, while Jacob was cooking some stew, Esau came in from the field utterly tired and famished. He was exhausted after a day of hunting which had little success. There were days like that, but Esau was particularly needy as he entered the tent this day. Seeing the pot on the fire, Esau asked his brother for some of the red stuff he was cooking. Jacob, as if he had been waiting for this moment, and sensing his brother's weakness, demanded that he first sell him his birthright, his right of inheritance. Esau, claiming to be at the point of death and not seeing any need for the birthright, agreed, but Jacob made him swear first, before he finally gave him the stew with some bread. As always, Esau gulped down the food and drank so quickly that by the time Jacob returned to the table, Esau had arisen and left. Thus Esau spurned the birthright which was rightfully his.

Just listen... Based upon Genesis 25:29–34.

The contrast between the brothers here could not be more vivid. Esau is a volatile individual who is caught up in the moment and in his physical needs. He is desperate for some of the "red stuff," the *adom,* that Jacob prepared. For this reason, Esau was also called by the name of Edom. Esau, the reddish one, the *admoni,* can only think about what comes from the ground. He is a man of the field who works outdoors, and his whole life is *adamah,* the land, the material, the physical. Like his predecessor Cain, he is tied to that which has been cursed. For Esau, the birthright, which represents concern for the future, is altogether unimportant. Both his personality and outlook are captured in the very staccato-like action words used at the end of the scene: *va-yachol, va-yesht, va-yakom, va-yelech, va-yivaz:* Esau ate, drank, rose up, left and spurned [the birthright].

He is desperate for... Genesis 25:25.

that which has been... Genesis 3:17.

va-yachol, va-yesht... Genesis 25:34.

Jacob is the exact opposite. He is pictured as shrewd, calculating, and concerned about his future status. Without any prodding from his mother, who later manipulates the stealing of Isaac's blessing, Jacob senses his brother's weakness and takes immediate advantage of him. He trades the momentary gratification from the food for the long term material benefits of the birthright. He knows what his brother needs, even craves, and barters some of the food which he concocted for future well-being.

Perhaps the story is not as simple and neat as it appears at first glance. After all, there is a striking irony here. Esau, the hunter, the one who provides food and sustenance for the whole family, is portrayed as literally "dying" for something to eat. And only his brother can satisfy his hunger. Listen to the story again. Esau, after a day of hunting, comes home exhausted.[12] He drags himself into the tent, falls down onto a chair and wants his brother, who has been home all day, to take care of him. He asks Jacob for some of the food that he has been preparing. What, in fact, does Esau want from Jacob? Or perhaps more to the point, what is it that Esau, the hunter, needs from the one who dwells in the tent? What is it that only Jacob can give his brother? What is it that each brother, and in this case each twin, needs from the other? Perhaps nothing less than what the "other" is and represents.

Each one holds the key to the other's sense of himself: In Jacob's case, the status and the future promise that comes with the birthright, and with Esau, his brother's caring, concern, affection, and place in the household. Esau is even called Edom because he craved the *adom*, the "red stuff," which Jacob had made. Esau is identified by that which he received from his brother. His entire being is caught up in who Jacob is and the differences between them. And so, however different, the two sides of the embryo are bonded forever. They are always to be measured and defined by the "other side."

We who have brothers or sisters know how siblings are tied to each other in this manner. We may have lived with the constant comparison with a brother or sister, and cannot forget how hurtful it was to be evaluated by who they were/are and what they achieved. Or worse, we, like Esau, may still crave to be like our brother or sister; to want what they have in their lives.

Isaac's Request of Esau:
Our Parents Are Often Dependent Upon Us

Esau's essential nature is also apparent in the story of the stealing of the blessing. You will recall the story begins when Isaac, quite old with his eyesight failing, orders his son Esau to go out to the field and hunt some game. He called Esau, saying, "My son," and Esau replied, "Here I am." Isaac told him that he was old, and did not know how much longer he had to live. He then asked Esau to take his gear, his quiver and bow, and go out to the field to hunt game and prepare the meat the way he liked it. In return, he promised to bless his son before he died. the story begins... Genesis 27:1–4.

This scene is all too familiar to each of us who has borne the responsibility of caring for an aging parent. We know the moment so well; it is our own test of faith. Isaac, tired and incapacitated, calls to Esau as he has done hundreds of times before. One more time, he calls to his eldest son and Esau responds with the classic *"hineini,"* here I am [ready to do for you]. The test of Esau, like ours, comes in an everyday, mundane context—when an elderly parent asks a child to prepare dinner. The challenge of *hineini*—whether we are ready to respond to those whom we love no matter how burdened we might feel—is sharply focused here. And in confronting Esau and his response, we confront ourselves.

For when his father calls to him imploringly, we feel for Esau. We feel the burden he bears as well as his desire to be there for his father. This comes through because a word is glaringly missing. When Isaac calls Esau, *"beni,"* my son,

[103]

why does Esau merely respond with *"hineini"*? In almost every case in the Bible in which a parent or child calls to the other using a term of familiarity, there is reciprocity.[13] Here, Esau does not reciprocate by saying, *"hineini avi,"* here I am, my father, and we understand why. Esau, who has been doing his father's bidding for a long time, naturally feels burdened. His father is dependent upon him and he is tired of the constant requests, especially in light of the very different expectations of his twin brother. And we who have cared for our parents recognize the tone of his ambivalent response.

My father, when he was ill and mainly confined to the house, needed help in order to be able to live on his own. Usually once or twice a week, I would visit him, take care of cleaning the apartment, and do some of his errands. Invariably while I was involved in one chore, like straightening up his bedroom, I would hear him call from the kitchen, where he sat by the window looking out onto the street below. His call, "Normyboy," would bellow forth, followed by a request that I go to the supermarket and shop for him. Such scenes were repeated weekly. And what was my response to his call? It was rarely ever one of joy or elation, such as "Sure Pop" or "Whatever you want Pop." More frequently it was something like, "Pop, I'm tired and it's late, and I have to get home." I almost always felt ambivalent (sometimes I recognized how ambivalent he must have felt being dependent upon me!), tired, and even angry. It was in such moments that I truly understood Esau's words—or in this case, his rather curt *"hineini."* This moment in the Genesis narrative is our moment and Esau's response forces us to weigh our own feelings and relationships with our aging parents.

But let us not be too harsh on Esau. As ambivalent, upset and even angry as he might have felt toward his father and his situation, he nevertheless responded positively, declaring his readiness to comply to Isaac's request. When all is said and done, he does say *hineini,* and perhaps in so doing, shows us the depth of his being. Even when feeling compromised and upset, he responds to his father. Of all the characters in the Bible, Esau is a model of *Kibbud Av,* honoring one's parents; he can teach us what it is to be a son or a daughter. Esau also helps us understand the importance of acting, irrespective of our immediate emotions and ambivalent feelings.

Esau is a model... Sifrei Devarim. *pisqa* 336, Bereshit Rabbah 65:16 and 82:14, and especially Devarim Rabbah 1:14.

The Hands of Esau and the Voice of Jacob: The Difficulty of Responding to All Our Children

When we looked at the the birthright scene, one of the most striking aspects is that even though Jacob and Esau are portrayed as utterly different, nevertheless, the closeness between the two brothers is also underscored. The same is true in the description of Jacob's stealing of Isaac's blessing.

For all their differences, the twins often sound and even act in the same way. When they approach their father bearing the food he has requested, Isaac asks each of his sons the same question and their responses are almost identical. It is as if they are one and the same person. It is no wonder then that Isaac found it almost impossible to differentiate between them, especially as Rebekkah had given Esau's clothes to Jacob to wear, and also placed the animal skins on his arms and neck.[14] And so when Jacob, dressed as his brother, approached his father offering the food his mother prepared, a seemingly confused Isaac blurts out in exasperation: "The voice is the voice of Jacob, but the hands are the hands of Esau." And the narrator adds that Isaac did not recognize his son and had to ask again, "Are you really my son Esau?"

Isaac asks each... Genesis 27:18–19 and 31–32.

as Rebekkah had... Genesis 27:15–16.

a seemingly confused... Genesis 27:22–24.

Even if Isaac were almost blind and perhaps a touch senile, as we are led to believe, is it really conceivable that he could not tell his sons apart? A blind individual compen-

almost blind... Genesis 27:1.

sates for his or her disability by listening more intently than the sighted person. Surely Isaac would recognize his son the moment he heard his voice. "The voice [was indeed] the voice of Jacob."

But there were other signs that it was Jacob who was standing in front of him. According to the dowry he had given Rebekkah when they married, Isaac had to provide her with two kids each day. The goat skins Jacob wore as well as the food she had prepared (in contrast to the venison that Esau would have hunted) were an indication to Isaac that this was Rebekkah's way of telling him that it was Jacob who was to receive the blessing.[15] It was Jacob, the younger son, of whom the oracle spoke when the two brothers struggled in her womb. We may, therefore, infer that Isaac was aware of the deception and chose to go along with it. As much as he loved Esau, Isaac would give Jacob the blessing. Isaac knew what he was doing and was aware of the consequences, especially given his subsequent conversation with Esau, which also shows he was in reasonable command of his faculties.

If Isaac did recognize Jacob, why then is he pictured as asking his son a series of repetitive questions about his identity? "Who are you, my son?" "Come closer that I may feel you, my son—whether you are really my son Esau or not!" "Are you really my son Esau?" These piercing questions have another purpose. When Isaac asks Jacob, *"Mi ata beni"* (Who are you, my son?), he is giving him the opportunity to acknowledge who he is and what he is doing, since the decision is already made as to who will receive the blessing. He is really asking, "What is your makeup?" "What is your essential nature?" "Are you Jacob or Esau, or both?" Like contemporary parents, Isaac simply does not know his son any more. He has manifested different qualities and has not acted in a consistent manner. Even though Jacob drew very close to his father, Isaac still wonders why the voice is

According to the dowry...
Bereshit Rabbah 65:14.

his subsequent conversation...
Genesis 27:33ff.

series of repetitive...
Genesis 27:18, 21, and 24.

When Isaac asks...
Genesis 27:18.

Jacob drew very close...
Genesis 27:22–23.

that of Jacob, but the hands belong to Esau. Isaac doesn't know him because he does not seem like Jacob: "And he did not recognize him because his hands were hairy like those of his brother, Esau."

It is not at all surprising that Jacob and Esau are confused here if we remember that they are twins, two sides of a whole, and appear both similar and different. They are symbolic sides of one and the same person: Everyperson.[16]

The text itself tells us that we have two sides of one entity here. For in response to Isaac's question, "Are you really my son Esau?" Jacob replies in a most unexpected way, "*ani.*" The word can be translated "I am," but perhaps it means, "It is I." The ambivalence and yet the unity implied by the word *ani* underscores the fact that Isaac is confronted by two very different characters, which are parts of a whole.

Nevertheless, it is precisely because Isaac responds openly when confronted by Jacob as he feigns being Esau that we can learn about the nature of relationship from him, especially we parents. Just listen again to the syntax of the phrase which Isaac utters: "Here I am; who are you my son?" Isaac may not know which of his sons is standing in front of him, yet he is open to whomever it is. It does not matter whether it is Esau or Jacob; he is there for both of them. This is the challenge that parents face every day if we are blessed with more than one child or are a part of an extended blended family. Even though we may have somewhat different feelings for each of our children and stepchildren, can we respond in a meaningful way to each one? Are we truly open to each one's particular needs and do we make ourselves available to them? Isaac is often characterized as being merely the son of the great father and the father of the great son—a generational transition between Abraham and Jacob. He is not thought to be very substantive, forceful, or important. Yet, in his response to Jacob we see him in a different light. He not only challenges Jacob's very nature by asking him, "Who are you, my son?" He also seems to love and respond to his children. He is ready to say *"hineini"* to both Esau and Jacob.

The Aftermath of the Blessing:
Identifying with Esau's Pain

It is not surprising then that Isaac is shaken when Esau returns with the food he has prepared. He is seized with a violent trembling when he has to confront Esau after conferring the blessing upon Jacob.

He is seized with... Genesis 27:33.

Yet, Isaac's pain cannot compare to that of Esau upon realizing he has been victimized by his mother and brother. Most of us who read the Bible pay little attention to Esau's anguish. After all, it is incidental to the theological agenda of the biblical writers of Genesis, who stress that Jacob carries the legacy handed down from his grandfather Abraham. But, if only this once, let us take time to listen to Esau. When Esau heard his father's words, he burst into wild and bitter sobbing and said to Isaac, "Bless me too, father!" But [Isaac], unable to tell his son the entire truth, answered him, saying, "Your brother came with guile and took away your blessing."[17] Esau then replied, "That is why he is named Jacob, for he supplanted me these two times. First, he took away my birthright and now he has taken away my blessing!" And he added, "Didn't you save a blessing for me?" "Have you but one blessing, father? Bless me too, father!" And Esau wailed aloud!

When Esau heard... Genesis 27:34–38.

If we had the impression that Esau was an uncouth hunter whose only concerns were his creature needs and who had himself to blame for his predicament, that surely is not the case here. His very human response elicits our sympathy and we see him as a deeply moving figure, the victim of a terrible plot.

Not only do our deep sympathies lie with Esau; if we are

honest with ourselves, we all can identify with him. Each of us who is one of several children in a family, or who has more than one child feels the hurt of a son who is deprived of his father's blessing. We have all been there in one way or another. We remember those times when we did not receive the expected affection or reward from our parents; or worse, that we knew in our hearts that our brother or sister tried to undermine our relationship with our parents. And how many times have we as parents been manipulated by one of our children to the detriment of another? Yes, Esau's painful words are our words: We have uttered them; we have heard them: "What about me, Dad?" "Do you only have time for my sister?" "Is there only one child important in your life?" Is it any wonder that we would rather ignore Esau's complaints and remain deaf to his cries? For to listen to them is to open ourselves to our own frailty.

We parents, like Isaac, sometimes think it is too late to make amends; too much has already happened to undo the unnecessary hurt. We can identify with the resignation in Isaac's voice when he responds to Esau's pleas for a blessing by saying, "But I have made [Jacob] master over you: I have given him all his brothers for servants, and sustained him with grain and wine. What, then, can I still do for you, my son?"

"But I have made... Genesis 27:37.

But Isaac does indeed have a blessing left for Esau. Yet in the process of blessing him, Isaac confirms Jacob's hegemony over him: "See, your abode shall enjoy the fat of the earth and the dew of the heaven above. Yet by your sword you shall live, and you shall serve your brother; but when you grow restive, you shall break his yoke from your neck." Yet, at the very moment when he underscores the differences between them—the older son shall indeed serve the younger, Isaac also gives each in part the very same blessing: They are to enjoy the dew of heaven and the fat of the earth. As different as the fate of the brothers shall be, they forever will be connected.

"See your abode... Genesis 27:39–40.

They are to enjoy... Note that Jacob is so blessed in Genesis 27:28.

[109]

Even Rebekkah, who loves Jacob and engineers the stealing of the blessing intended for Esau, links the two siblings in a most unexpected way. When she hears that Esau plans to kill Jacob once their father dies, we can imagine how desperate she feels. Overcome with the image of one of her sons killing the other, she counsels Jacob to flee to Haran, to Laban's house, in order to save his life. But in urging him to stay away until Esau's anger subsides, she expresses her fears that if he does not, she will "lose the two [of them] in one day."

But in urging him...
Genesis 27:45.

The terror of the moment is clear to Rebekkah. If Esau kills Jacob, he in turn will become a fugitive and she will lose him as well.[18] The problem is that up to this point Rebekkah has expressed no affection for Esau and in reality is already distanced from him. Might we surmise that these words indicate that Rebekkah indeed did love her firstborn son Esau? Perhaps that is the reason that the text curiously emphasized that Rebekkah kept Esau's best clothes with her in the house. It is possible, though not probable, since Rebekkah and Esau really never interact, either before this incident or afterwards.[19]

Rebekkah kept Esau's...
Genesis 27:15.

Yet, Rebekkah is afraid of losing both sons, no matter how much or little love she feels for Esau. As twins, from their conception, they have been umbilically tied to each other and to her. The struggle between the two in their mother's womb tore her apart. Could the death of Jacob at the hands of Esau have any less of an effect? Esau and Jacob are two sides of a whole she helped create, and the death of one would be tantamount to the death of both. How could she live with that pain for the rest of her life? How would it be possible for her to bear both the guilt for her own actions and the loss of her future at the very same time? For the first time, Rebekkah was as much the mother of Esau as she was the mother of Jacob, and now she stood to lose both of them.

Mahanaim: Two Camps—
Having to Face Our Other Side

In order to prevent the loss of her son(s), Rebekkah insists that Jacob flee to her brother Laban's house in Haran. Had Jacob not left Canaan, Esau surely would have killed him once Isaac died, since he seemed consumed by hatred. The two brothers would not only live a great distance apart during the next twenty years; the tie between them appears to have been totally ruptured. And we can only surmise what impact the intervening years, while Jacob worked for Laban and Esau remained in Canaan, might have had upon their feelings toward each other.

Rebekkah insists... Genesis 27:41–45.

However wide the chasm, twenty years later Jacob found himself on a journey homeward; one that involved confronting Esau. As he draws near his destination, he is met by a band of angels and thinks to himself, "This is God's camp" (*mahaneh Elohim*). As a result, he names the place *Mahanaim,* "Two Camps." Why does Jacob choose the name "Two Camps" and not "God's camp"? What or who are the "two camps?"

he is met by... Genesis 32:2–3.

It is clear that from the very outset, even prior to sending gifts to Esau and dividing his camp in two in order to protect his family and possessions, Jacob focuses our attention on the conflict. There indeed are two camps—Jacob and Esau, the two sides of one whole. And it is Jacob himself who makes the symbolism clear to us, when he implores God just a bit later: "And now I have become two camps. Please deliver me from my brother, from the hand of Esau." His brother Esau is the "other camp," his other side.

implores God just ... Genesis 32:11–12.

So what choices does Jacob have as he is about to confront the Other in his life? Why should we expect Jacob to be any different than we are? When confronted by that part of ourselves with which we struggle, our own shadow(s) or perhaps our sibling(s), we are quite adept at erecting protective defenses.

Jacob sends messengers... Genesis 32:4–5.

And so Jacob "sends messengers ahead of him to [greet] his brother Esau," calling him "my lord" and referring to himself as his brother's servant. Jacob's intent is spelled out by his own words: It is his hope to gain Esau's favor. Yet, he clearly does not mean any of it. But it was to no avail, at least as Jacob understood it, since he is told that his brother was marching toward him accompanied by a band of four hundred men. Although Esau's intentions are not clear (perhaps he meant his brother no harm and his entourage is simply a way of greeting Jacob), the fact is the news added to Jacob's anxiety, and he is forced to prepare for the worst.

He divides his possessions... Genesis 32:8–9.

He divides his possessions into two separate camps, thinking that if Esau attacks one camp, the other will be able to escape. Often when we confront our brothers or sisters, or the repressed dark side of ourselves, our hope is not to come to some greater sense of wholeness and peace. If you are like me, you have anticipated many conversations with a sibling with the simple desire to cut your losses and merely survive the moment. We do not expect to solve difficult conflicts, but rather to move beyond them with as little damage done as possible.

Divided into *"mahanaim,"* two camps, and thinking that he faced eventual conflict with Esau, or perhaps with himself, Jacob even resorts to turning to the God of his ancestors. This is the first time that he prays. Interestingly, Jacob's words are reminiscent of the greeting he sent to Esau, as he

"O Lord, who said... Genesis 32:10–11.

asks God to fulfill his earlier promise to him: "O Lord, who said to me, 'Return to your native land and I will deal bountifully with you. I am unworthy of all the kindness that You have so steadfastly shown your servant....Deliver me, I pray, from the hand of my brother, from the hand of Esau.'"

Perhaps, Jacob's willingness to turn toward God and admit he is unworthy of God's kindness indicates the beginning of his maturation.[20] However, Jacob seems simply to be invoking God's protection as he faces his brother. He will even manipulate God if he has to in order to survive!

As Esau comes toward him, Jacob, now quite desperate, realizes he has to appease his brother if he can. We ourselves know this tactic well. By giving in to our other side just a bit, by feeding the shadow of ourselves, we hope it will disappear. Jacob selects large numbers from his herds, sending them in droves to his brother and instructing his servants to tell Esau they are gifts from Jacob, who is following behind. He stations himself behind in his familiar defensive posture. And Jacob reasons to himself: "If I win him over with presents in advance, and then face him, perhaps he will show me favor." Jacob did not understand that Esau would not be appeased by gifts. If we are to reconcile with the other side of ourselves, it will only happen if we are willing to embrace it. Our brother cannot be bought off!

Jacob selects large...
Genesis 32:14–19.

Jacob reasons to himself...
Genesis 32:21.

The Fording of the Jabbok:
Can We Overcome That which Divides Us?

For all of his defensive strategy, Jacob found himself alone on the bank of the Jabbok River. For some unknown reason, he arose in the middle of the night and sent his whole family and all his possessions across the river, while he alone remained on the other side. And it was there, at *Ma'avar Yabbok*, at the point of crossing the river, whose letters were simply the inversion of Jacob's own name, *Ya'akob*, that the struggle for reconciliation actually began. As he lay staring up at the stars, alone with his thoughts and his fears, Jacob took the first step toward bridging the split in himself. The Jabbok was to be Jacob's Rubicon!

he arose in the...
Genesis 32:23–24.

And as he lay there, consumed by recollections of his brother, Esau, and what had happened between them, a man appeared who began to wrestle with Jacob. Perhaps the man was a part of a dream, or maybe someone actually had forded the river under the cover of darkness and attacked him. As the story was told and retold, some said that the *ish*, the man with whom Jacob struggled, was an angel. After all, the text tells us that "Jacob struggled with the divine and the human, and prevailed." Just as Jacob had encountered the angels upon the ladder at Beth El, at the beginning of his journey, so, too, he met an angel here, at Mahanaim, near the Jabbok River, upon his return from Laban's house.

"Jacob struggled with...
Genesis 32:29. The identification of the man as an angel is based on Hosea 12:4–5.

Yet, both moments could represent Jacob's own struggle with his higher self, with the divine within. They were part of his journey toward wholeness. Jacob's struggle at the Jabbok was to reconcile his two sides, the god-like and the human. Jacob confronted Jacob that night—the deceiver faced the son of Isaac and the grandson of Abraham, the progenitor of the Twelve Tribes; for the man appeared as a shepherd, possessing flocks of sheep, goats, cows and camels; the very animals Jacob had brought with him from Haran. And the man said to him: "I will help you take your animals across, then you can help me with mine." The two shared a similar goal (future?) yet they would up end up fighting with each other.

the man appeared...
This is based upon Bereshit Rabbah 77:1–2 and other midrashim.

Perhaps Esau himself had forded the Jabbok during the night, taking advantage of his brother's vulnerability in order to revenge the theft of his blessing. In his dream that night, Jacob pictured Esau as an angel coming from the west,[21] for when the battle was ended, he called the place *Peniel*, meaning, "I have seen a divine being face to face." The next day, when he encountered Esau in the light of the morning sun, he similarly remarked, "To see your face is like seeing the face of God." And as Jacob wrestled with Esau in the soft earth on the riverbank, and as their blood intermingled with the mud, they reenacted the struggle in their mother's womb.[22] They fought throughout the night, under the darkness of a moonless sky, as they had inside

Jacob pictured Esau...
See Bereshit Rabbah 77:3 and 78:3 among others.

he called the place...
Genesis 32:31. Subsequently, the place is referred to as Penuel.

Rebekkah; they fought until the first rays of sunlight began to break through.

And when the night figure saw that he could not prevail against Jacob, he desperately wrenched Jacob's hip at its socket in an attempt to overcome him. Indeed, the blow should have weakened Jacob, enabling the man to free himself. But it only seemed to strengthen Jacob's resolve.[23]

So his opponent pleaded with Jacob to let him go, to which Jacob responded, "I will not let you go unless you bless me!" Jacob still needed the other's blessing. Though some twenty years has passed, he had not forgotten how to capitalize on the other's vulnerability. Years before he had won Esau's birthright by taking advantage of his brother's desperate need for food. Had Jacob changed at all?

Jacob already had been given Esau's blessing, yet he needed to receive it again. Perhaps what he needed most was to be given it by Esau himself, not merely to receive it from his father as he had earlier. We, like Jacob, may have gotten much recognition from those we have loved, including our parents. Yet, deep down, what we need the most is the recognition and love of those whom we have hurt. Like Jacob, we need to feel that those we hurt in the past still love us. Jacob struggled with Esau from the very beginning, and stole the birthright which was rightly due his older brother. Therefore, it was all important that Esau bless him.

Yet Jacob was confused. From the moment at Mahanaim, when he thought he had encountered God's angels, the *malakhim*, Jacob found himself at the same time sending his own *malakhim*, his messengers, to Esau bearing gifts. He could not easily distinguish between the divine and the human. On that very day, he had implored his brother to treat him with mercy, as a servant would entreat his master, but in almost the same breath, Jacob prayed to God to act mercifully by delivering him from his brother's hand.[24] Perhaps Jacob's fear of Esau as well as his feeling of guilt helped

"To see your face...
Genesis 33:10.

he desperately...
Genesis 32:33.

him to see that his struggle was not merely with his brother. It was also with the other side of himself, the divine within or in the world. As a result, he names this place of struggle *Peniel,* saying that "he has seen God (or a divine being) face to face."

he names the place...
Genesis 32:31.

Seeing Esau's face was indeed tantamount to seeing the Divine. And so, in response to Jacob's demand for a blessing, the wrestler renamed him "Israel" explaining, "For you have striven with the divine and the human and you have prevailed." Indeed, Jacob had struggled with both—with himself and with this other side, whether it was his brother Esau or that which was God-like in him. And he had survived. Perhaps he had even begun to change and grow; to integrate the conflicting sides of himself.[25]

Seeing Esau's face...
As Jacob actually says when he meets Esau the following day. See Genesis 33:10.

"For you have...
Genesis 32:31.

Jacob was different! He was transformed by the encounter with the figure on the bank of the Jabbok. As the sun rose in the eastern sky, Jacob could be seen coming from the direction of Penuel and his night encounter. He was walking with a noticeable limp. Jacob had been irreparably wounded in the struggle making him even more vulnerable to attack from Esau. However, the word for limp is *tzoleiah,* which is similar to the term *tzelah,* meaning "side" or "rib." In the story of Creation, God's removal of Adam's rib is the moment of birthing of his other side. Here Jacob is transformed and is now ready to be reconciled with the other.

Jacob could be seen...
Genesis 32:32.

In the story of...
Genesis 2:21–22.

That is precisely what is most odd. Though clearly weaker, Jacob's more vulnerable demeanor allowed Esau to see him differently, perhaps more sympathetically. And similarly, Jacob would approach his brother with a wholly different attitude.

The Moment When Brothers Meet:
Transforming Our Own Relationships

The next day, as Jacob limped away from Penuel, he raised

his eyes and saw Esau approaching from a distance, accompanied by the band of men his messengers had reported. In anticipation, Jacob once again divided his retinue, placing the handmaids and their children first, followed by Leah and her children and then Rachel and Joseph. But this time, Jacob did not take up the rear, protecting himself as he had done the previous day. Rather, he himself went on ahead, even though he may have still feared Esau might kill him. Perhaps for the first time, Jacob was willing to put himself on the line as he paid his elder brother the respect he deserved. As he moved forward toward Esau, Jacob bowed low to the ground seven times until he was close to his brother. Jacob acts contrary to one who possessed the blessing and the birthright; he finally was willing to humble himself before Esau.

Jacob once again...
Genesis 33:1–2.

as he had done...
See Genesis 32:1, 19.

Jacob bowed low...
Genesis 33:3.

How do brothers greet each other after twenty years of separation? Who would be willing to take the first step; to utter the first words? Every family has lived through such moments: Brothers or sisters estranged, perhaps even harboring hatred for each other, dreading the moment when they will have to confront each other again. And in that instant when we first glance at each other, when we see our brother or sister for the first time in a long time, we feel the pain/the joy of the moment of reunion. Conflicts with our siblings, with the other sides of ourselves, are not irreconcilable. Separation can be overcome and integration is possible, as we see in this moment of encounter between Jacob and Esau.

After Jacob had bowed before his brother, Esau ran to greet him. How could he hold back? This large bear of a man, so volatile and deeply emotional, could not restrain his feelings. After all, Jacob was his brother whom he still loved, despite everything that had transpired. Esau had thought for a long time about this moment and wondered how he would react. But now there were no feelings of ha-

Esau ran to greet...
Genesis 33:4.

tred, jealousy, or revenge. All he could focus on was how much time had been lost; much of the past had been forgotten. And so he ran toward his brother, the same one with whom he had wrestled from the beginning, in real life and in his dreams. They had struggled in their mother's womb, but now he found himself running towards Jacob with arms open wide.[26] It was indeed possible to move from conflict to unity; from struggle to embrace.

Instead of striking his brother, Esau embraced Jacob and, falling upon his neck, kissed him. Tension had always existed between them, especially after Jacob stole Esau's blessing. Esau had wanted to kill him. And even by the bank of the Jabbok River, Jacob and he struggled throughout the night. Now they were clenched, not in a wrestling hold, but rather in an embrace.[27] From a distance it is difficult to tell if one is witnessing two people fighting or hugging. It is possible to transform a stranglehold into an embrace. What it takes is the will to overcome the disparate forces within us and outside of us and become a better functioning whole. And the starting point is our ability to recognize that it is our brother or sister or ourself who stands over and against us, the one to whom we have been attached from the very beginning.

to come together... Genesis 33:4. Perhaps it was the struggle with the Divine-human figure the previous night, the feeling of closeness, of bonding they experienced that allowed Jacob and Esau to come together now in an affectionate embrace. We might have expected Esau to fall upon Jacob and attack him. Instead, he places his head upon his shoulder and kisses him.[28] Esau embraced his brother with a whole heart. He indeed had missed him and he still surely loved him. It is difficult not to be touched deeply by this scene as the two brothers cry in each other's arms.

And then, just as Jacob had raised his eyes and had been struck by the sight of Esau being accompanied by his large entourage, Esau now looks up and sees Jacob's large family and many possessions. (It is surprising when these two brothers—twins—who seem so different, occasionally respond in very similar ways. Or is it?) And when Esau asks Jacob who they are, Jacob replies that they are "the children with which God has favored your servant." God truly graced him with a large family, but he nevertheless is finally willing to see himself as Esau's servant! As his fate has been in God's hands, he knows that his fate now rests with his brother.[29] As his wives and children come forward to greet Esau, Esau is concerned about his brother's intent as he approaches with this large company. Jacob says simply that it is all "to gain my lord's favor." Not only does Jacob refer to Esau as his "lord" after calling himself Esau's "servant," but now he seeks Esau's favor, as he has benefitted from God's favor. For Jacob, the struggle with his brother had always been a struggle with the divine.

This could not be any more explicit than when he pleads with his brother: "No, I pray you; if I have found favor in your eyes, accept from me this gift, for to see your face is like seeing the face of God." The same word *hen* (favor) is used by Jacob when he refers to Esau and to God. The struggle with our sibling, with our other side, is also the struggle with our higher selves, that impulse in us which makes us transcend our human natures.

"No, I pray you... Genesis 33:8–10.

But how can we overcome the fragmentation and better integrate our different sides? How is it possible to overcome the separateness? Perhaps only by giving up the insulated defensive postures we habitually assume and reaching out to find acceptance, as Jacob began to do with his brother. He had to be ready to give of himself, sacrifice a part of his ego, if he was to be reconciled with Esau. And he does. He implores Esau to take the gift he has brought so that he will find favor with him. When Esau asks him about the large company or camp, the *mahaneh,* by which he is surrounded,

When Esau asks him... Genesis 33:10.

Jacob replies that he wants to gain Esau's favor, *hen,* by offering him a *minhah,* a gift.[30] In anticipation of his meeting with Esau, Jacob had readied for battle by dividing his retinue into two armed camps, *mahanaim.* Yet, the conflict dissipates and instead of attacking or being attacked, Jacob offers his brother his gift—his *minhah*—a sign of affection and love; a symbol of reconciliation.

But Jacob knows what it is that he must give up if he is to repair his relationship with his brother; if he is to move toward a sense of completeness in his life. At this moment of meeting, he must give back to his brother that which he stole from him some twenty years before—Esau's rightful blessing. And the text comes full cycle as Jacob then begs Esau: "Please accept my present *(birkhati)* which has been brought to you; for God has favored me and I have plenty." His *minhah,* his gift to his brother, is his *berakhah,* the blessing he possesses; the one which he is guilty of taking. We now understand why Jacob rather desperately implores Esau. His gift is meant not only to propitiate his brother, but more importantly to atone for his sinful actions.[31]

"Please accept...
Genesis 33:11.
See also Midrash
Sekhel Tov to
Genesis 33:11.

Jacob had grown enough to want Esau to take back the *berakhah* that was rightfully his. He no longer needed Esau's blessing. And after much urging, Esau accepts it. In so doing, Esau finally was able to embrace his younger brother. Jacob had given up that which was not his in the first place; Esau was able to let go of the anger he had harbored for these twenty years and the pain that he bore alone. He finally had embraced his brother in love, and Jacob responds by saying, "You have received me favorably—*va-tirtzeni.*"[32]

**and Jacob
responds...**
Genesis 33:10.

The two sides, which had been in conflict, were together as they had never been before.

The Journey from Penuel:
After Coming Together, We Often Move Apart

The solidification of the relationship between the brothers seems to have been achieved. Jacob had given of himself to Esau—a gift/his blessing—and his brother had embraced him, as only a sibling can. Esau, for his part, was ready to ride off together with Jacob and begin their lives anew. He thought to himself, "I have only one brother and I love him above all else. I have no other sibling in the entire world, but him. We were together in our mother's womb, and came forth at the same time. He is part of me as I am part of him. If I don't love Jacob, whom shall I love? How wonderful it would be for us and our families if we were to live together in Seir. 'Let us [then] start on our journey.'" Desiring nothing more than being with his brother, Esau adds, "I will proceed alongside of you *(le-negdekha)*."[33]

' **Let us then...** Genesis 33:12.

Esau had forgotten the past, and all the pain. He simply thought that although they were so different, they surely could live together in harmony. If it had been up to him, they would have travelled as one family to Seir.

But Jacob remained wary; or perhaps he, more than his emotional brother, understood that the hunter and the shepherd can never really live together, as much as they might care for each other. How could Jacob explain that to Esau? How could he tell him that it just would not work; it wasn't meant to be! Similarly, how can we say to our brother or sister that as much as it is nice occasionally to spend time together, and have our children get to know their cousins better, it really isn't feasible for us to spend the entire summer together. Spending that much time in such close proximity would simply not work. We are too different and set in our ways to be able to live together for any length of time.

But instead of being open and forthright—he never

really had that ability—Jacob once again manipulates his brother. And Esau, for all his success these many years, still can be easily handled. So Jacob replies, first arguing logically that his children are young and weak, and the flocks and herds must be driven slowly, lest they not survive the journey. Falling back to a defensive posture that always felt more comfortable, Jacob asks that Esau move on ahead of him and promises that he will eventually get to Seir at his own pace. We already know that Jacob has no intention of travelling there.

The moment of rapprochement which took place west of Penuel, a bowshot from the Jabbok River where Jacob had wrestled in the night and as a result began to bridge the fragmented parts of his life, was suddenly over. And as Esau started back on his way to Seir, Jacob journeyed toward Sukkot and Shechem.

One can only surmise what was going through Esau's mind as he turned to glance at Jacob's company moving slowly behind him. In his heart of hearts, did he know that the only time he would see his brother again would be at their father's burial in Hebron, Kiryat Arba, as Isaac and Ishmael had come together one last time to bury their father? Had he noticed at all that Jacob's entourage had begun to turn slightly westward and not east to Seir? Or was he oblivious to the reality of who they were and how their destinies were different? Maybe in his naivete he actually thought that Jacob would arrive in Seir, ready to build together for the future.

Although Esau may have had visions of their life together as he moved away from their meeting, Jacob was already making his way to the city of Shechem, where he arrived *"shalem."* We assume that the biblical writer is telling us that Jacob came to Shechem *in peace.*[34] After all, he had survived his encounter with Esau who had threatened to kill him after the stealing of the birthright. Little does Jacob

So Jacob replies... Genesis 33:13–14.

as Esau started... Genesis 33:16–17.

at their father's... Genesis 35:29.

or the reader know that his sojourn in Shechem will be anything but peaceful. He would soon experience the rape of his only daughter Dinah and witness the slaughter of the Schechemites in retaliation.

experience the rape...
Genesis, Chapter 34.

Perhaps the description of Jacob as *"shalem"* means that he was "whole." However, we cannot escape the irony, for Jacob is pictured as having been wounded in his encounter at the Jabbok. But that seems to be the point: Physically Jacob was fragile, but spiritually he finally has integrated the disparate parts of himself.

But if we think that Jacob's transformation was complete, we are immediately dissuaded by his silence in the face of the events surrounding the rape of his daughter in the ensuing narrative. In order to underscore that the change in Jacob was not complete, the biblical writer continues to call him by that name even after the angel changed his name to Israel. Indeed God has to appear to him later on to remind him who he is/still can become: "Your name shall no longer be called Jacob, but Israel is your name"; real change is very slow, even arduous, and although we may be in touch with the different shadows that we possess, we find that there are times when we are unable to control them and channel them in constructive ways. Similarly, for Jacob the struggle to become Israel was not over.

the biblical writer continues...
Genesis 35:9–10.

Jacob continues to live with the different sides of himself, as symbolized by the distance Jacob and Esau have moved apart after their fateful meeting. To be sure, they see each other again at their father's burial. Just as Ishmael and Isaac before them, they stand as brothers in the field and pay their father their last respects. And as if the biblical writer were trying to show us just how close the two were, at that moment he describes their respective family constellations. If we compare their genealogical trees closely, we see clearly their similarity. The genealogies of both Israel (Jacob) and Edom (Esau) come from four matrilineal

four matrilineal...
Genesis 35:23–26 lists the sons of Jacob, while Genesis 36:10–14 recounts the sons of Esau using the same matrilineal guide.

Esau took his...
Genesis 36:6–8.

Esau settled in...
Genesis 37:1.

lines and their respective numbers are about the same.

However, lest we believe that there was a full reconciliation between Jacob and Esau, the text immediately emphasizes that the two brothers could not yet be united. As they had to separate from the womb, so, too, they now could not dwell in the same place. Esau took his wives and his children and all that he possessed and went into a land far away from his brother, Jacob.[35] Their substance was too great for them to dwell together; and the land in which they sojourned could not bear them both. Esau settled in the hill country of Seir, while Jacob lived in the land where his father had resided, the land of Israel.

The brothers, the shadows of each other, two sides of one whole, the shepherd and the hunter, could not live as one. Each would have to continue to stand alone. And so like his predecessors before him—Cain, Lot, and Ishmael—the ones who could not inherit the birthright, Esau travelled eastward, *kedmah,* to Seir, leaving Jacob to fulfill the covenant that was tied to the land of Israel.

Like Jacob and Esau, we too might become reconciled with our siblings, the other side of ourselves, yet that moment of understanding will not necessarily last forever. Reconciliation does not always mean unity or identity, at least in a world that is not yet Eden.

CHAPTER FIVE

LEAH AND RACHEL

Seeking My Sister; Finding Myself

As we look at the story of Rachel and Leah, we see rivalry and conflict that extend throughout their lives from the moment Jacob enters their father's house. The two sisters vie for Jacob's affection as they try to solidify their own positions by providing him with progeny for the future.

Nevertheless, Rachel and Leah, who could not be any more different, are similar in that each one constantly measures herself by the other's relationship with Jacob. In the end, however, the two sisters become united in a way that we never anticipate. The bonding of the two is achieved when each is able to reach beyond herself and show concern for the other. By giving up their own power, they find each other and in the process themselves.

Does this merging of opposites only happen in the biblical stories, or can it be achieved in our lives? Can we reshape the relationships with our siblings? Can we bridge our own fragmentation and come to a greater sense of wholeness?

After their reunion, Jacob watched Esau and his retinue move on. As his brother disappeared in the distance, what kept rushing through Jacob's mind was the image of Esau running toward him that day in the fields near Penuel, enveloping him in a bear hug, and kissing him. Glancing at his wives, Rachel and Leah, Jacob also recalled that his long sojourn in his uncle's house had begun in the same way, with Laban running towards him, embracing and kissing him.[1] The two individuals in his life with whom he had the greatest conflicts had greeted him in the same affectionate manner!

Esau running toward...
Genesis 33:4.

with Laban running...
Genesis 29:13.

As he mused, he began to realize that the two experiences—his struggle with his brother and the competition set up by Laban between his wives—were much the same. His conflict with Esau, his deception of his father Isaac, his stealing of the birthright and blessing of the firstborn, and the flight from his father's house were all mirrored in the events in Haran. If he had realized this when living under Laban's roof, trying to survive amidst the tension and pain, things might have turned out differently. Maybe not. Perhaps what happened was the result of the inevitable tensions among siblings in each generation, or the conflict inherent in the different sides of our own personalities. Simply put, the struggle between Leah and Rachel was a repetition of the conflict between himself and Esau.[2]

Are we any different than Jacob? Caught up in interpersonal conflict, with our spouse, child, parent or significant other, we often realize we keep repeating the same experiences over and over. We become unhappy when we recognize that our ways of responding to others have not changed over the years. We all know those moments when we hear ourselves say things to someone we love that we swore we never wanted to say again, but we cannot stop ourselves. And we wonder if we will ever be able to do so. Like us, Jacob was upset at the thought that he still survived by manipulating others. Like Jacob, we must internalize what we have learned from past experiences if we are to alter our behavior.

Jacob Meets Laban's Two Daughters: Recognizing Our Different Personalities

Jacob also reflected on how little he had anticipated what would transpire at the watering hole that day when he approached Haran and his uncle's house some twenty years before. While he spoke to several shepherds waiting with their flocks by the well, Laban's younger daughter moved towards them from a distance. He was overcome by the sight of this woman, his own flesh and blood, leading her father's flock. Not only was she very beautiful, but unlike most women of the day she was able to take care of her father's sheep.[3]

While he spoke to... Genesis 29:4–9.

leading her father's flock... Genesis 29:9.

Her name, Rachel, seemed quite fitting—the little ewe; indeed, as he came to know, she possessed the strength and the patience of the shepherd as well as the softness and vulnerability of the sheep.[4] He saw and responded to her different sides: Perhaps they mirrored the shadows of his own persona.

Her name was Rachel... Genesis 29:10–11.

Jacob surely was moved deeply by his meeting with Rachel, expresssing more emotion at this moment than at any other time in his life. He kisses her and raises his voice, crying out unabashedly. Jacob is no different than any of us. It usually takes one special person to bring out the best in us. When we encounter and come to know a Rachel, we somehow are able to tap into hidden resources that have gone undeveloped. Through our relationship with this special person we can become who we truly are.

He kisses her... Genesis 29:11.

Laban, on hearing the news that his sister's son had arrived from the land of Canaan, rushed to greet and embrace Jacob, calling him "my bone and my flesh." Jacob

rushed to greet... Genesis 29:13–15.

[127]

almost seems to have escaped one antagonist, Esau, only to encounter another who took his place. In fact, Laban refers to Jacob as his brother, saying, "Just because you are my brother *(ahi)*, should you serve me for nothing?" For the ensuing score of years, while working for his uncle, Jacob struggled with Laban in a way reminiscent of his conflict with Esau.

Sometimes things are not as simple as they seem. Who is the manipulator and who is manipulated? Do we end up having done to us as we do to others? Here we see that Jacob would be the pawn in the tension between Leah and Rachel. Although at this point he is bartering with Laban for wages, it is he who will become the object which is bartered by his two wives. When he hears Laban saying, "Tell me, what shall be your wages," he does not know that later Leah, having exchanged her mandrakes for the right to sleep with him, will chide Jacob, saying, "I have surely hired you with my son's mandrakes." Jacob, the conniver and manipulator, will be manipulated by both Laban and his own wives.

At first glance it seems that Leah and Rachel are the objects which Jacob and Laban are trading. Note the flow of the text here: [Laban says], "What shall your wages be?" which is followed immediately by the words, "Now Laban had two daughters; the name of the older one was Leah, and the name of the younger one was Rachel." Not only Rachel, but also Leah would be Jacob's possession. They would surely share the same fate, as we have come to expect with siblings in our story.

Although we seem to know nothing more than the fact that they were sisters, stories handed down over the generations about their similarity circulated amongst the people. Some even believed them to be twins. That they often act as parts of a whole—two sides which complement or parallel each other—therefore should not be surprising.

Yet, from the outset, the two were also described as being

"Tell me, what shall...
Genesis 29:15. Laban used the word *maskurtecha* (your wages), which is based on the root *sachar.*

saying, "I have surely...
See Genesis 30:16 below. The Hebrew is *"sachor sacharticha."*

"What shall your wages...
Genesis 29:15–16.

Some even believed...
According to Sefer ha-Yashar 23:28, Adinah, Laban's wife, conceived and bore twin daughters.

totally different. Listen to the Genesis text again: "Now Laban had two daughters; the name of the older one *(ha-gedolah)* was Leah, and the name of the younger *(ha-ketanah)* was Rachel. Leah had weak eyes, but Rachel was shapely and beautiful."

Perhaps Leah was fittingly described as having *einayim rakkot,* weak eyes, since her very name, Leah, means weak or tired.[5] And over the course of time a legend grew that Leah's eyes indeed were weakened and she herself became weary from weeping over her fate. For when she and her sister were born, her father, Laban, had arranged with his sister, Rebekkah, living in Canaan, that their two firstborn children, Leah and Esau, would one day marry, as would their younger offspring, Rachel and Jacob. But when Leah heard of the kind of person Esau was, she prayed to God, beseeching, "May it be Your will that I do not fall to the lot of that wicked man."[6] Leah's eyes were weak because of her deeply sensitive nature.

Perhaps this is why people said Leah's eyes were *rakkot,* since the Hebrew word more typically means delicate or soft. While Rachel was outwardly beautiful, certainly more physically attractive than her sibling, Leah was sensitive and kind—tender of spirit. The sisters represent two different natures—two distinct forms of beauty, and Leah's purity of spirit is deemed more substantive.[7] Indeed Rachel, the beautiful one, was barren, while Leah, in contrast, was very fertile. Rachel, who later stole her father's household idols, is appropriately described here as barren, "being void" of concern and sensitivity.

The emphasis upon Leah's substance in relation to Rachel also explains the words used here to describe their status in the family: Leah was the *gedolah* (the older one), while Rachel is called the *ketanah* (the younger one). In contrast to other descriptions of the sisters, in which Leah is correctly referred to as the *bekhirah* (the first born) and Rachel

"Now Laban had... Genesis 29:16–17.

she herself became weary... See Bereshit Rabbah 70:16, Tanhuma ha-Nidpas, *Va-Yetze* #4, Bereshit Rabbati to Genesis 29:31, and B.T. *Baba Batra* 123a.

who later stole... Genesis 31:19.

Leah was the gedolah... Genesis 29:16.

other descriptions...
For example,
Genesis 29:26.

the *tzeirah* (the younger), the terms *gedolah* and *ketanah* could refer here to their natures. Leah is clearly the one with "greater" spirituality. Rachel is the "lesser" of the two.

The difference between the sisters should not surprise us, since we know that surface beauty is often deceptive. We, like Jacob, however, are frequently enticed by what our eyes see and hearts feel, as opposed to that which our minds and souls can appreciate. We, too, are taken in by surface traits and rarely ever probe more deeply.

The Deceiver Is Deceived:
We All Must Wake Up to Reality

It is not surprising therefore that Jacob would be attracted by Rachel and not by Leah. From the first moment that he laid eyes upon Rachel at the well, he fell head over heels in love with her. And the text emphasizes the fact that he was

Leah was weak/ soft...
Genesis 29:17–18.

smitten by her beauty, noting that "Leah has weak/soft eyes, but Rachel was shapely and beautiful; and Jacob loved Rachel." Jacob probably hardly noticed Leah or recognized her caring, good nature. All he desired was Laban's younger daughter, his *ketanah,* and offered to work for seven years in order to acquire her as his wife.

Perhaps Jacob, so caught up with Rachel's physical presence, did not need or care to know much about her. For seven years, he simply longed for her to the point where his body ached. He memorized every curve, every inch of her body. He often recreated her in his mind's eye as he lay in his bed at night and dreamed of the day when he would have her. For all we know, Rachel may have entertained the same fantasies as she contemplated her future husband. But we know that Jacob yearned to make her his wife. He must have counted the days, weeks, and months until Rachel would be his. When the seven years were up, he impatiently demanded of Laban: "Give me my wife, for my time is ful-

For seven years he...
Genesis 29:20.

"Give me my wife...
Genesis 29:21.

filled, that I may lie with her." In his eyes, Rachel was the object for which he had worked all these years. Now it was Laban's turn to fulfill his end of the bargain.

For Laban, too, his daughters were objects of barter. The night of Jacob's wedding, after a large feast celebrating his union to Rachel, as Jacob lays waiting in their marriage bed, Laban tricked his son-in-law by substituting Leah for Rachel. And Jacob slept with Leah, thinking Rachel shared his bed. How was it possible that he could be fooled? After residing in Laban's house for seven years and counting the days until he finally would make Rachel his wife, why wasn't he able to tell with whom he slept? Did he not know the sisters at all, or was he simply so self-involved that he could not distinguish one from the other? What is known is that in the morning light, Jacob was aghast when he saw Leah.

after a large feast... Genesis 29:22–23.

Perhaps we should not be surprised. After all, Jacob himself had succeeded in usurping his brother's blessing by tricking his blind father only years before. Now, in the darkness of his tent with Leah's face likely covered with a veil (as his neck and arms were disguised by the animal skins), Leah took her sister's place. In essence, Jacob was as blind as his father. Just as Jacob convinced Isaac that he was the firstborn child, so Laban substituted his firstborn as Jacob's wife. And just as Jacob stole the blessing because Isaac's eyes were weak, so weak-eyed Leah became his first wife.

in the morning... Genesis 22:25.

Is Jacob's vulnerability so surprising to us? Have we not wondered how it is possible that we fall prey to the very traits and acts which we have witnessed in relation to our parents and criticized? Each of us has thought many times that once we become parents, we would never do the things our parents did to us! But there is more here. When we're honest with ourselves, we'll even admit (if we are at all self-aware) that our kids act towards us the very same way we acted towards our parents, and they, like us, get away with it. We are as vulnerable to our children as our parents were to us, and things have a way of coming full circle. So it is that Jacob gained the status of the firstborn and then, to his chagrin, married the firstborn daughter of Laban.[8]

Jacob's fate vis à vis Laban's two daughters was set by his actions with his own father and brother. The deceiver was now the one who was deceived, although Jacob doesn't seem to understand the connection between the events, as he incredulously exclaims to Laban: "What is this that you have done to me? Did I not work for Rachel for you! Why did you deceive me?" Ironically, his father Isaac had used the same term in describing his actions to his brother Esau: He said: "Your brother deceived me and took your blessing."

We all know individuals like Jacob. It might be our own son or daughter, our own sibling, or even ourselves (though we most probably would not realize it). It is the person who is quick to complain about how he or she is being treated, all the time failing to understand that he or she is guilty of the very same behavior. It is the child who pouts about her brother who would not lend her a toy, yet never is comfortable with sharing what she has with others. Why is it that we criticize in others what are sometimes the very traits we possess?

So it is that Jacob, now tricked by Leah and Laban, is reminded in no uncertain terms by his uncle about his past acts: "It is not the practice in *our* place to marry off the younger before the elder." Laban in effect is telling Jacob that "It might have been the custom in your place to give the younger child precedence over the firstborn, but it simply isn't done that way here!" In Canaan, Jacob, the younger son, could manage to receive his father's blessing, but this father—Laban—would follow the custom of marrying off his older daughter first.

With all of this, we have not asked how Leah and Rachel felt about the sudden turn of events, or for that matter what it was like to live in their father's house under the same roof

"What is this that...
Genesis 29:25. The term for "deceive" in Hebrew is *rimitani,* from the Hebrew root *rmh.*

"Your brother deceived...
Genesis 27:35. The word *mirmah* (guile or deceit) is based on the same root as *rimitani.*

"It is not the practice...
Genesis 29:26.

as Jacob for these seven years. While Jacob was eagerly awaiting the time when he would marry Rachel, how did the two sisters relate to one another? What did Jacob's feelings, the impending marriage, and the intrusion of their cousin into their lives mean to them? How did Leah survive knowing Jacob desired Rachel? Did it only confirm her sense that she wasn't beautiful and would never attract a man? And worse, what was she to do when her father took her aside at the wedding feast and ordered her to ready herself to take her sister's place? Did she desperately try to dissuade her father, worrying what this would do to her sister, or was she quietly eager to be the one whom Jacob would wed? After all these years of feeling rejected, she would lie with Jacob and be his wife. But in the morning, she, as well as Laban, would have to face Rachel. What could she possibly say that would ameliorate her sister's pain?

Each one of us who has a sibling knows that moment when we have faced our brother or sister, when one of us was hurt by our parent who gave unexpected and perhaps unwarranted preferential treatment to the other. Surely those of us blessed with children must have done the same more than once, causing one of them much pain. Sometimes parents do try to compensate, however inappropriately, when we perceive one of our children needs special attention, despite the unfairness and the tension it engenders. Many times, we even think our actions are justified. And in the light of morning, as they face us and each other just as their matriarchal forebearers did, what can they possibly say to one another? Could Laban have acted any differently given his family's situation? Can we as parents forestall conflict among our children by better anticipating how what we do will affect them?

What would make matters worse and complicate the situation even more was Laban's promise to give Rachel to Jacob following the seven day bridal feast if he would serve him

Laban's promise to... Genesis 29:27.

another seven years.[9] Not only would the sisters have to live under the same roof as wives of the same man, but they would do so both knowing Jacob's preference and remembering the way in which Leah had joined with him. For the forseeable future, they would share the same husband, if not his affections.

The Struggle between Leah and Rachel: How Can Siblings Be So Similar and Yet So Different?

Although Leah and Rachel shared a husband, both sisters were convinced that Jacob loved only Rachel. However, was this really the case? Our sole indication about how Jacob felt is that we are told that "he, indeed, loved Rachel more than Leah." Jacob clearly felt more for the younger of the two sisters, but Leah is not despised nor rejected. We do not hear of Jacob's indifference to Leah; he never says anything about how he feels towards her, nor is he willing to forego his relationship with her in deference to her sister. Jacob simply loved them both, albeit feeling more passionately for Rachel. This, in fact, might have aggravated the situation. Knowing that Jacob loved each of them—perhaps in different ways—could only serve to make the sisters' relationship more contentious. What lay ahead was seven years of strife as each sister/wife would vie for her husband's attention and love.

Yet, even though Jacob did possess genuine care and affection for Leah, in her heart of hearts she thought that Jacob only really loved her sister. After all, she knew how attracted he was to Rachel and how she was the one for whom he was willing to work. No matter how many times Jacob might have shown her that he cared for her, Leah must have continued to feel rejected, even perhaps despised.

We, too, can sometimes sense that one of our children seems to feel unloved or unappreciated, no matter how much we pay attention to him or her. That child is convinced that we love our other child(ren) more, even though it might actually be a case of loving our children in different ways. This is particularly true in families in which there are both children and stepchildren. Often, it is impossible for our spouses' children to feel that we care for them in any deep way. It is so obvious to them that our true affections rest with our "real" children. Having helped raise my wife's son and daughter, with whom I have lived since they were eight and eleven years old respectively, I often think about their deep-seated feelings toward me and the extent to which they may feel some resentment because of my relationship with my own three children.

Yet, not only they, but our "real children" experience the same feelings among themselves. I am sure that my own three children occasionally think that I love their brother or sister much more than I love them. What can I or any parent do to counter such erroneous perceptions? How can we convince our children that what they perceive to be greater love is simply the result of how they see and interpret our actions? Is there any more to be done than to act in the most consistent manner possible, with the hope that they will grow and mature so as to be able to see our true intentions?

Like them, Leah's feelings did not go unnoticed. Although Jacob may not have looked at her in the same way that he looked at Rachel, and as a result she may have felt tremendously insecure, jealous and unworthy, there was a power in the universe in whose eyes she could find favor.[10] God saw how bereft Leah felt and helped her realize her own worth and power by enabling her to become pregnant. She would be the wife who would bear Jacob's children. Once again, we are struck by the sharp contrast drawn between the two sisters. Leah, the sibling with the weak eyes, though not as attractive as her sister Rachel, was perhaps softer and more sympathetic as well as more fertile. It is

God saw how... Genesis 29:31.

poignant that Rachel, who was physically more beautiful, at this point was incapable of having children. Leah, the more compassionate one, had her womb opened by God, while Rachel remained barren.[11] The sisters appear almost diametrically opposite, two very different individuals physically as well as emotionally. Taken symbolically, Rachel and Leah, like their counterparts, Jacob and Esau, represent the contrasting sides of each of us. As we witness their competition, we become more in touch not only with our own conflicts with our siblings, but with our inner struggles as well. We, too, can at times be warm, compassionate and giving, and at other times, cold, empty and hard. The struggle between these two sisters forces us to confront who we are.

God indeed was aware of Leah's pain and caused her to conceive and bear Jacob's firstborn son. She named him Reuben, since God had seen her affliction.[12] Now, she believed Jacob would love her. Providing him with a male heir would seal their relationship. When she conceived a second time, she became even more convinced that God had heard her cries. She therefore named this second son Shimon, emphasizing that "God heard [her] pain." And after bearing her third son, she felt Jacob would surely be attached to her, so she named the child Levi. Actually the name means "to accompany [someone]", but usually for a short period of time. Perhaps Leah knew in her heart of hearts that although Jacob was supremely happy about the birth of his three sons and felt close to Leah as a result, he still loved Rachel deeply.

Nevertheless, when her fourth child was born, she named him Judah, thereby praising God and acknowledging God's power and goodness. How powerful that Leah is portrayed as the one having an ongoing relationship with God.[13] Only later and very briefly is God pictured as responding to her sister. Unlike her older sister, Rachel never is described as praising God. Leah is grateful and expresses her thanks to

had her womb opened...
Genesis 29:31.

She named him...
Genesis 29:32.

When she conceived...
Genesis 29:33.

She felt Jacob...
Genesis 29:34. The name Levi is based on the Hebrew root *lavah*. See, in this regard, Bereshit Rabbah 71:2.

when her fourth child...
Genesis 29:35.

God, as she has every reason to do. After all, she has provided Jacob with four sons, proving her worth and insuring the clan's future. She does not know of course just how crucial her progeny will be; that the line of Judah will eventually lead to King David and the messianic.

How the situation has changed. Leah, who felt unloved, even hated, has become the guarantor of future generations. And all this time, her sister Rachel has remained silent.

line of Judah... See the Davidic genealogy at the end of the Book of Ruth.

Rachel Responds to Leah's Success: Seeing Ourselves in Contrast to Our Sister or Brother

Who we are should be the reflection of our own talents and limitations. But how often do we define ourselves in relation to the "other"? So it is with Rachel and Leah. Until now, we know absolutely nothing of Rachel's feelings. Perhaps she is totally devoid of them; she is *akarah*, barren, as we have been told. Yet, having experienced the birth of her sister's four sons, and realizing that she has not provided Jacob with any children, she became envious of Leah and demanded of her husband, "Give me children or I shall die!" All Rachel can see is that her sister is fertile and presented her husband with four sons, and that as a result, her relationship with Jacob is in jeopardy. If we did not know better, we might have thought that it was Leah who mouthed these words. Here Rachel sounds just like her sister prior to the birth of her children. Rachel, too, seems insecure, jealous and self-deprecating. Only through bearing children can she feel whole and fulfilled.[14]

"Give me children... Genesis 30:1.

It is also clear that she, like Leah earlier, can only see herself in light of who her sister is, as she is caught up in the battle for progeny and her husband's affections. We could even imagine Rachel saying to Leah: "I had his love, but you had the fruit, so there was a kind of justice. But now, you my sister will have it all, the love and the fruit, and I shall eat dust!"[15] Each side of this pair of siblings is defined by her counterpart and constantly struggles with her.

If we are honest with ourselves here, Rachel's response is quite painful to us—most probably because deep down we know these feelings of jealousy and insecurity. We have felt at times, especially in our youth, inferior to a brother or sister, and most probably expressed it inappropriately. We yelled at one of our parents or took it out on another sibling, but we rarely ever expressed our feelings directly since we were not even all that conscious of them. Our own children have acted in similar ways. How many of their actions are the result of how they feel vis à vis our other children? When one child heard that his brother or sister had gotten excellent grades for the semester and he was able to get only C's no matter how hard he tried, his negative self-perception resulted in biting and angry comments towards everyone. We experience inappropriate behavior in our families all the time, but we do not always recognize its source.

Jacob Does Not Understand Rachel's Pain: Can We Respond to Those Whom We Love?

Rachel, in her anger and jealousy, not only appears almost identical to Leah here; she also reminds us of Jacob. When she impulsively demands, *"Havah li banim"* (Give me children), she echoes Jacob's explosive impatience when he demanded of their father Laban, *"Havah et ishti"* (Give me my wife). It had to be difficult for Jacob to hear these words. Could this be the Rachel whom he had deeply loved all these years and who was the object of his affections? How could she turn on him so? And besides, why did she seem to place the onus on him? After all, he was the father of four children and if she had not conceived, whose fault was it?

Angered by Rachel, Jacob retorts, "Can I take the place

When she impulsively...
Genesis 30:1.

when he demanded...
Genesis 29:21.

"Can I take the...
Genesis 30:2.

of God, who has denied you the fruit of the womb?" Jacob seems totally oblivious to Rachel's pain; he doesn't realize how difficult it had been for her to witness the birth of his four sons while she remained infertile. But how can this be? Living under the same roof and sharing her bed, how can he be so insensitive and uncaring? All he is capable of is denying his own responsibility and placing the blame on Rachel, and by extension the Divine. How different from Leah who raised her voice praising God for providing her with children.

Leah who raised... Genesis 29:35.

Jacob's angry response to Rachel is not unfamiliar. We all know couples who are faced with problems of infertility and the strain that it places upon their relationships. Feelings of frustration, anger, defensiveness, and guilt are all typical in these situations. The desperate demand of Rachel and the inappropriate reaction of Jacob could have been voiced by someone we know, a person to whom we are close, or even by our spouse or ourselves. Nevertheless, just as we hope that we would be more understanding when confronted by our spouse's pain, or of someone we love, so, too, we expect more of Jacob since he claims to love Rachel deeply.

The Sisters' Conflict Continues through Their Handmaids: We Struggle to Love Others; We Struggle to Love Ourselves

Struggling to hold on to her husband's love in the face of her sister's fertility, Rachel gives her handmaid Bilhah over to Jacob in an effort to provide him with a son from her.[16] Like Sarah, she can only compete with her husband's other wife and feel valued if her handmaid were to bear a son. As she indicates to Jacob, it is the birth of a son that will literally build her up, as it did her sister Leah.[17] Both Leah and Rachel think that bearing a child will raise their status and

Rachel gives her... Genesis 30:3–4.

It is the birth... Genesis 16:2.

solidify their relationship with Jacob.

When Bilhah conceives and bears a son for Jacob, Rachel exclaims, in a tone and words reminiscent of Leah, "God has judged me *(danani)* and also has heard *(shama)* my voice and given me a son." Therefore she named him Dan.[18] Even though both she and Leah emphasize that God heard their pleas, Rachel cannot name her child Shimon or a variation thereof, since Leah has already given her second child that name. The two sisters act in almost identical ways and their lives are continually intertwined. They are locked in as intense a struggle as their cousins, Jacob and Esau.

This is most evident when Rachel's handmaid conceives again and gives birth for a second time. Upon seeing the child, Rachel exclaimed: "I have been engaged in a God-like struggle *(naftulei Elohim niftalti)* with my sister and I have prevailed." Rachel therefore named her second son Naftali. Echoing through Rachel's words is the description of Jacob's struggle at the Jabbok with his counterpart: "You have struggled with the Divine and the human, and you have prevailed." Rachel prevailed over her sister just as Jacob would prevail over Esau in his struggle.

Like her husband Jacob, Rachel was able to overcome the other side of herself, her shadow, and become whole.[19] The tension and strife between the two sisters is summed up in this one dramatic remark by Rachel, but at the same time it powerfully recalls the similar stories of self-struggle throughout Genesis. Just as these biblical characters, we wrestle with all that is within us, in hopes of prevailing—overcoming our fragmentation and integrating the disparate elements in us.

The conflict between Leah and Rachel should not be surprising, however, since they, like the other siblings in the stories in Genesis, have much in common. Now that Rachel's handmaid has provided Jacob with two sons, Leah, who just a few short years before felt that the bond between herself

"I have been engaged... Genesis 30:8.

"You have struggled... Genesis 32:29. The verb used—*yachol*—is the same in both stories.

and her husband was firm and secure, can only think about one thing—that she is no longer able to bear children. All that she can see is her barrenness, just as her sister Rachel several years before had been envious of her.[20] Each one is defined by the other.

What was Leah to do? Like Rachel earlier, she decided to give her handmaid Zilpah to Jacob to regain his love and admiration. Not only do both sisters give their maids to their husband, but Zilpah like Bilhah, Rachel's handmaid, conceived twice in a short period of time and bore two sons, Gad and Asher. Once again feeling vindicated and even triumphant, Leah exclaims: "What luck...What fortune!...Women will deem me fortunate." The shifts in the fortunes of the sisters within the story and the constant role reversals only serve to underscore further the ongoing dynamic and tension between these two symbolic sides of every person. As different as they are, the two sisters experience their conflict in similar ways, just as each of us vacillates between feelings of control and vulnerability. In this light, the only question we think about here is how Rachel will react to Zilpah's bearing two additional sons for Leah. Though Rachel thought she had prevailed over her sister, it is clear that she will have to do something drastic if she is to retain Jacob's love.

but Zilpah like...
Genesis 30:10–13.

Bartering Over the Mandrakes: Can the Relationship between Siblings Change Over Time?

A short time later, while Leah's firstborn Reuben was helping to bring in the wheat harvest, he came upon mandrakes in the field and brought them to his mother. In his concern for his mother and her seeming inability to have any more children on her own, Reuben gave her these flowers, believed to be an antidote to barrenness as well as an aphrodi-

Reuben was helping...
Genesis 30:14.

siac.[21] When Rachel saw what Leah's firstborn son had collected for her, she rushed to her and pleaded for some of the mandrakes. She desperately needed some of Reuben's *dudaim*. Rachel desired what her sister had—both Leah's fertility and the very close relationship she had with her firstborn. Maybe she means: "Please give me some of your son's *dudaim*—your son's love and affection."[22] Whatever Rachel desires, we know how important it is to her as well as to her sister, when Leah exclaims: "Was it not enough for you to have taken my husband, that you would also take my son's mandrakes?" Rachel's desire for the mandrakes is seen to be as crucial in Leah's eyes as her winning Jacob's affection.

"Was it not enough... Genesis 30:15.

The balance clearly has tipped in Leah's favor. She now enjoys a position of power, perhaps as never before in her relationship with Rachel. Her sister is forced to give up the one thing that she has been able to hold on to all these years, her access to Jacob. All this in order to gain what Leah possesses—her son's mandrakes, her fertility, the fact that she has four sons of her own, and the status that this entails. And so Rachel promises Leah that Jacob will lie with her that night in return for the mandrakes.

And so Rachel promises... Genesis 30:15

When Jacob comes in from the field, in a scene reminiscent of the time when Esau returns from the field only to be tricked by Jacob, Leah rushes out to meet him and says: "You are to lie with me for I have hired you *(sachor sechartichah)* with my son's mandrakes!" This surely is not the quiescent, vulnerable and self-deprecating Leah whom we have encountered before. *Va-tetze Leah*—Leah went out to the field to meet him, as Rachel had gone out to shepherd the flock many times in the past.[23] The roles seem to be reversed as Leah behaves much more like her younger sister.

Leah went out... Genesis 25:29 and 30:16.

And if the relationship between the sisters has changed, so has Jacob's relationship with them. One can only wonder what Jacob thought when Leah advised him that he was her "hireling" that night. After all, when he first came to Laban's house, his uncle had given him his daughter Rachel as his "wages" *(maskoret)* and seven years later Jacob demanded payment. Over the course of his stay in Haran, he had gone from the barterer to the one being bartered. The exchange between Leah and Rachel here also reminds us of the incident between Esau and Jacob over the birthright. In both, an established right is given up for a desired vegetable substance: Esau sells his birthright for a pot of lentil soup, while Rachel exchanges her "right" to lie with Jacob for Leah's mandrakes. Jacob, who takes advantage of his brother's desperate hunger and as a result his willingness to give up his status, is here the very object being bartered. As Esau could only think of his immediate gratification, so, too, can Rachel. The irony, of course, is that not only does Jacob become the object being bartered, but Leah's actions remind us of his own behavior toward Esau—both seem in control and take advantage of their siblings.

his uncle gave...
Genesis 29:15.

Just when we seem to have a handle on one or all of the characters, and on the way the siblings interact, they change on us. As sides or shadows of the symbolic whole, we should not be surprised when they act in completely contradictory ways. We, too, occasionally behave in very different ways, exhibiting our contrary sides. Yet, we derive hope that we can bridge the sides of our own natures from the coming together of Leah and Rachel.

Leah and Rachel Come to Wholeness: Gaining Strength by Giving of Ourselves

Jacob did indeed lie with Leah that night, although Leah harbored very little hope that she would conceive, since she had given her mandrakes to Rachel. She had been infertile for some time, but that did not matter. She had Jacob to herself once again.

[143]

God had recognized... See Genesis 29:33 in this regard.

she conceived and... Genesis 30:17.

She named her... Genesis 30:18.

Little did she know that in giving up her mandrakes and their promise of new life, she had gained in the process. As God had recognized her plight in the past, heard her pain, and then opened her womb, so now the Divine heard her inner thoughts, and she conceived and bore a fifth son for Jacob. God was again responsive to her as the Divine had not been to Rachel. And this is even more powerful now since Rachel was the one who possessed the aphrodisiac.

God had indeed rewarded Leah ("God gave me my *sachar*") and therefore she named her newborn Issachar, because she had bartered away her mandrakes *(sachar sechartichah)*. She gave up something that was to give her power, the mandrakes, and in turn became empowered. In her greater wholeness, she was able to experience the gift of creating a new life again.

This powerful moment in the text is all too familiar to many of us today who struggle to conceive a child. We either have experienced it ourselves or know of couples who have done so. When people desperately want children, sometimes nothing that they try seems to help. They have utilized every kind of mandrake, but to no avail. Occasionally, when the individuals simply are relaxed and comfortable with themselves and their relationship, when they feel a sense of wholeness and bonding, they unexpectedly experience the miracle of childbirth.

But there is much more here that is important, even for those of us who have never faced problems of infertility. As we try to become "new" ourselves, the notion that by giving up something that seemingly will give us power we can become empowered is a challenge we must face. The conversation between Oskar Schindler and Amon Goeth, the commandant of the Plaszow Labor Camp in the movie *Schindler's List,* in which Schindler tried to convince the German officer that by not using the obvious power he possessed, he would be seen as being even more powerful, haunts us. Do we really believe it and have we the strength to actualize it in our lives and relationships? Can we who need to feel in control and enjoy exercising the power of our office or our position learn to act in the exact opposite manner? Can we alter the way in which we relate to those of significance in our lives, thereby finding our true selves and greater happiness in the process? The story of Leah and Rachel teaches us that we have no choice but to struggle with these challenging questions.

In the process of bearing another son, Leah felt the power of creating a new life surge through her body and became assured of her place in Jacob's life. And when she immediately conceived again, she knew that God, in giving her this gift, had guaranteed her future. After all, she had provided Jacob with six sons, half of the twelve tribes of Israel. She named her sixth son Zebulun, for the bond between her and her husband Jacob would last forever.[24]

She named her sixth... Genesis 30:19.

But Zebulun was not the last of Leah's children. After his birth, we are told that she also bore a daughter named Dinah.[25] A story circulated among Jacob's clan that Dinah's birth was miraculous. Supposedly Leah was informed by the oracles that she was carrying a boy in her womb, which would have given her seven sons while her sister had only one of her own. Feeling secure in herself and in her relationship with Jacob, she now empathized with her sister's predicament for the first time. Leah prayed earnestly for a girl, asking that God would alter the sex of the child in utero. Leah's piety and caring, long recognized by the people, is clear here and her prayer is the first step toward dissipating the tension between the two sisters. The battle for Jacob's affection and their place in the family hierarchy seems to be over. The sisters, apparently so different, are now moving toward a greater sense of unity and integration.

she also bore a... Genesis 30:21.

Supposedly Leah was informed... See B.T. *Berakhot* 60a and Targum Yerushalmi to Genesis 30:21 among others.

According to the story, it was Leah's prayers which insured that Rachel gave birth to as many sons as their two handmaids. Since Leah had given up her mandrakes as well as the possibility of birthing a seventh son, God heard her and blessed her with two more male offspring. Similarly, Rachel had sacrificed the only thing that gave her power in her relationship with her sister—access to their husband Jacob.[26] As a result, as the Divine had remembered Leah several times before, God again heard her prayers. By sacrificing something of themselves, each sister gained. As God had opened her sister's womb years before, so the Divine opened Rachel's womb and she felt the exhilaration of new life inside of her for the first time. And she cried out: "God has removed my disgrace"; so she named her newborn Joseph, adding, "May the Lord add another son for me."[27]

God again heard...
Genesis 30:22.

"God has removed...
Genesis 30:24.

The sisters were finally equals; both had provided Jacob with a blessing for the future. Rachel bore Joseph with the promise of a twelfth son, Benjamin, a son for Jacob's old age, as Leah had provided him with his firstborn.

Challenges for the Future:
Learning to Live Together in a Family

We are left with the problem of not knowing which of Jacob's two wives is more valued or which of his sons is the guarantor of his people's future. To be sure, Leah's son Reuben is the first of the tribes, as is mentioned in several places. Yet, Reuben sinned by sleeping with Rachel's handmaiden Bilhah and was punished. In addition, Joseph was Jacob's favorite; he loved him more than his other sons, as he had loved his mother Rachel. And Joseph received the richest of blessings from his father at the end of his life. Jacob surely considered Joseph his real heir, the hope for the future.[28]

as is mentioned...
E.g., Numbers 1:20.

Rachel's handmaiden...
Genesis 35:22. Reuben's punishment is alluded to in the enumeration of Jacob's blessings in Genesis 49:3.

blessings of his father...
Genesis 49:22–26.

The fact that Joseph was the favored son made absolute sense, since Rachel was the apple of Jacob's eye. It was as if she were his true wife, while Leah was simply the mother of some of his children.[29] When Rachel, his favorite, dies on

[146]

the road near Ephrath in childlabor, Jacob sets a pillar to mark her grave for posterity. Leah's death in contrast is not even recorded in the biblical story. All that is reported is that Jacob buried her in the Cave of Machpelah. While Rachel would be mourned throughout the generations, Leah disappeared from the narrative. Perhaps her death did not have to be marked, since the two sisters had become united as never before. The sibling rivalry had dissipated and the two sides were now one.

on the road near...
Genesis 35:20.

buried her in the...
Genesis 49:31.

Yet, the fact that Leah, not her sister Rachel, is buried next to Jacob in the Cave of Machpelah gives us pause. Leah would be together with Jacob in death as perhaps she never was in life. The two lie next to one another in perpetuity. She inherited the coveted position, while Rachel who had died prematurely birthing Benjamin was laid to rest on the Bethlehem road.

Moreover, for all the glory Joseph attained, it was Leah's progeny who provided Israel with priesthood and prophecy—Moses and Aaron come from the tribe of Levi—and with royalty—David stands in the line of Judah, leading to the messianic. While Joseph and Benjamin, Rachel's sons, enjoyed their father's affections, the future of Israel would be determined by the children of Leah, both in terms of sheer numbers as well as leadership. The enduring link between the generations of Israel would extend from Leah through the House of David.

As we pass from the pairs of siblings—Jacob and Esau, and Leah and Rachel—to the generation of their children, it is not surprising that tension still exists. Rachel's sons stand over against their half brothers, the sons of Leah, and the struggle between them is immediately evident in the continuing saga of the family/nation. This leaves us wondering if our conflict with our own siblings and with the shadows of our own personalities can ever be totally resolved. Can we truly repair our relationships and thereby experience a greater sense of wholeness in our own lives? Is it possible to ever regain the unity we once knew in the garden?

❙ ❚ ❙

CHAPTER SIX

JOSEPH AND HIS BROTHERS

The Two Sides Meet Again

From the moment of his birth, Joseph was bonded to his younger brother Benjamin. Rachel's two sons would struggle all their lives with the sons of Leah and the sisters' two handmaids. Not unlike children in blended families today, Jacob's sons had to wonder if the distance and tension between them could ever be overcome.

Could the same brothers who sold Joseph into slavery regret their actions, admit their guilt and even come to love Joseph? Would Judah, Joseph's rival, act differently if he were given a similar opportunity to show his concern for Benjamin? Could he demonstrate greater responsibility than he had when he did not fulfill his obligations to his daughter-in-law, Tamar?

These not only are questions we ask concerning Joseph's (and Benjamin's) relationship with the other ten sons of Jacob, but they are also our questions. What will it take for us to learn to act differently and do we have that capacity? Can we ourselves change over time so that when we are confronted with difficult situations we have mishandled in the past, we will act more maturely? Can we learn to step up to responsibility?

Joseph's life was bound up with that of his brother, even though Benjamin would be born years later. Their mother Rachel sealed their united fate when she gave her firstborn son the name Joseph, as she petitioned God for another child: "May the Lord add another son for me."[1] Joseph and Benjamin would stand as one against the sons of Leah. And indeed Joseph was set apart from Jacob's other sons.

For once Rachel had provided Jacob with a guarantor of the future, Jacob was ready to return to his father Isaac's house to claim his place as the rightful possessor of the birthright and the blessing. In Jacob's mind, Joseph was the link in the chain of the tribe's destiny, the one upon whom its future would depend.

Joseph's emotional separation from his stepbrothers began when Reuben, Leah's firstborn, slept with Bilhah, his father's concubine. Reuben took what belonged to his father and at the same time violated Rachel's handmaid. To Jacob, Reuben seemed to have declared that he was ready to displace his father, to claim his birthright as the firstborn, while for Joseph, Reuben had blasphemed the memory of his mother who only recently had died. Distraught, Joseph ran to his father to tell him what his older brother had done.[2] Joseph, who later would be identified as a talebearer, knew exactly what his father's reaction would be. Jacob would remove the birthright from Reuben, who had profaned his bed. Perhaps Joseph hoped that it would become his. As a result of informing his father of Reuben's sinful act and Jacob's rejection of Reuben, Joseph's brothers began to despise him, especially Reuben's natural brothers—Shimon, Levi, Judah, Issachar and Zebulun, who felt rejected too.

Joseph was isolated. His mother had been buried on the road to Ephrat, and his brothers wanted nothing to do with him.

All he really had in the world was his infant brother, born as his mother gasped her final breaths and whom she called

gave her firstborn son...
Genesis 30:24.

Jacob was ready...
Genesis 30:25.

slept with Bilhah...
Genesis 35:22.

identified as the talebearer...
Genesis 37:2.

remove the birthright...
See 1 Chronicles 5:1 in this regard as well as Sefer ha-Yashar 36:15.

buried on the road...
Genesis 35:19.

gasped her final...
Genesis 35:20.

Ben Oni, the son of my affliction. Jacob, not wanting his newborn son to bear the grief of his mother's death all his life, renamed him Benjamin, "son of [my] right hand." Benjamin, and his brother Joseph, born through Rachel, the object of his father's love, were Jacob's preferred sons. They became intimate friends who shared a common fate, even though born years apart. Benjamin was the extension of Joseph, the second son for whom Rachel had longed when Joseph was born. The very ambiguity in his naming at birth points to the shadowy role he would play throughout the family's story.

Our situations are no different than Jacob's, since the special bond between Joseph and Benjamin is obvious to any of us who live in large families. This is especially true in a blended family. As parents and stepparents, we know the pain of seeing our children and stepchildren pair off as if they live in armed camps, while we try desperately to bridge their differences. And children who have grown up in such a family know where their deepest loyalties reside. I vividly recall the first time my wife and I took our five children (when we met, the children ranged in age from 2 to 7 years old; I had three and my wife had two) away for a long weekend. It was only a matter of hours until the lines were drawn and we had to play referee the entire time. We simply hoped to survive the three days. The question constantly faced is whether such alignments in an extended family can ever be overcome.

The Object of His Father's Love and His Brothers' Hatred: How Our Relationships Break Apart

Joseph's preferred position in the family and his isolation from his brothers is evident from the outset of the story of Jacob's family in Canaan. "Now Jacob had settled in the land in which his father [Isaac] had resided, the land of Canaan.

"Now Jacob settled...
Genesis 37:1–2.

This, then, is the line of Jacob." This is the story of the twelve tribes who would become the people of Israel. And just when we expect the text to review in chronological order Jacob's progeny, beginning with Reuben, the firstborn, and continuing with Leah's sons, we read instead: "Joseph, who was seventeen years old, tended the flocks with his brothers." Joseph was the heir to his father's position in the line that began with Abraham and continued through Jacob: "This, then, is the line of Jacob: Joseph was seventeen...." The future of the family is totally focused upon Joseph, as it was upon his father. And as Jacob had produced twelve sons who became the twelve tribes of Israel, Rachel's son also should have produced twelve tribes. Although Joseph only had two sons, Ephraim and Manasseh, his brother Benjamin had ten sons, all of whom bear names that have something to do with Joseph's life. Together, Joseph and Benjamin are the brothers who provide Rachel (and Jacob) with twelve heirs, just as Jacob had for his father.

There indeed is a closeness between Joseph and Benjamin, as if they are the same entity and cut from the same cloth. We are told, for example, that Joseph enjoyed a special relationship with Jacob because he was Jacob's *ben zekunim,* the son born to him in his old age. Yet, we know that Benjamin, Jacob's youngest son, was born to Rachel after the family had returned to the land of Canaan. In fact, later on in the story, Benjamin himself is referred to as Jacob's *ben zekunim.*

That Joseph would spend all his time with the sons of the handmaids, Bilhah and Zilpah, and dwell in the same tent as Benjamin, is not at all surprising.[3] After his mother's death, Bilhah became a surrogate mother to both Benjamin and Joseph, and he grew close to her. Contrastingly, the sons of Leah treated him as an intruder, never having a good word to say to him. Benjamin was too young to notice the disdain that was palpable to Joseph.

his brother Benjamin...
Genesis 46:21. See also Bereshit Rabbah 84:5 as well as Yalqut Shimoni 1, *remez* 46, 150.

he was Jacob's...
Genesis 37:3.

Benjamin himself...
Genesis 44:20.

with the sons of...
Genesis 37:2.

Joseph alienated his brothers even more by the way he acted in the fields as they shepherded their father's sheep, as if he could lord it over them, "lead" them as it were.[4] And he was all of seventeen. He constantly told them what to do and how to act. What made matters worse, he frequently gossipped behind their backs. He returned from the fields filled with tales about what they had said about their father in order to ingratiate himself even more with Jacob.[5] Jacob accepted it completely. In spite of Joseph's actions, or perhaps because of them, Jacob came to love Rachel's son even more; more than all the others. And he set him apart from his brothers by giving him an ornamented tunic, a veritable coat of spendid colors; a *ketonet passim,* a striped coat. It was the very coat Leah and Rachel had worn on their wedding nights, and originally had been presented to Reuben as Jacob's firstborn.[6] The heads of tribal clans, royal princes and princesses, typically wore such magnificent, colorful garments. Following Reuben's terrible sinful act with Bilhah, Jacob stripped him of the coat and kept it until Joseph came of age. Now Joseph was ready to assume his rightful place as the one who possessed Jacob's birthright. As Jacob placed the coat upon his shoulders, he could feel the power that finally was his.

Joseph knew that Jacob loved him more than all his brothers, and so did the brothers. When they saw how their father treated Joseph, they grew even more jealous. They hated him so much that they could not bring themselves to speak a kind word to him.[7] They found it difficult even to mention his name. But the breaking point came with Joseph's outlandish dreams of superiority that he readily shared with them. The dreams, the images of their sheaves bowing down to his sheaf, or worse, the sun, moon and eleven stars all bowing down to him, gave his siblings a clear picture of how Joseph saw himself—as the leader ruling over them.

came to love...
Genesis 37:3.

heads of tribal...
2 Samuel 13:18 as well as Aggadat Bereshit, Chapter 61.

Jacob stripped him of...
Sefer ha-Yashar 36:15.

the dreams, the images...
Genesis 37:5–11.

The fact that *all* the brothers came to hate Joseph is quite astounding, given that they were divided among themselves. They were divided into clans that probably had little to do with each other. The sons of Leah, on the one hand, and those of the handmaids, Bilhah and Zilpah, on the other, stayed for the most part to themselves. Only Joseph spent time with the children of the handmaids. Yet, Joseph's arrogance and disdain served to unite his stepbrothers. This fragmented group of envious and resentful siblings together turned on Joseph as the object of their hatred.

Joseph, the shrewd schemer, seemed oblivious to how his words and actions galvanized the emotions of his brothers. So caught up in his dreams of grandeur, which masked his feelings of aloneness and vulnerability after his mother Rachel's death, Joseph could not see the extent to which his brothers, even the sons of Bilhah and Zilpah who had been his friends, were aligning against him.[8]

The story of Joseph is the story of the brother or sister who is disliked by all the other siblings because his or her insecurity causes him or her to be overly boastful, loud, demanding and generally obnoxious. It is someone many of us are acquainted with. It might be one of our own brothers or sisters who was the focus of our entire family's energy when we were growing up, or more painfully it might be one of our children. Those of us who live in blended families are keenly aware of how the feelings our respective children have of being left out and alone are responsible for their irritating behavior. At times, we too may have seen how our other children all appear to resent and vent their anger upon this one child, who frequently has no idea why she is being treated so unfairly by her siblings. He or she feels especially hurt since all he or she really wanted to do was to help them, love them, and be loved in return.

However, the most difficult realization for us as parents in this situation is that we ourselves have built up similar kinds of negative feelings toward this same child. We too have felt the resentment well up inside and occasionally heard it spew forth in angry words. We, like our other children, have felt manipulated, belittled, and spoken to in ways that a child simply should not treat a parent.

Joseph Responds to His Father's Request: The Power of Hineini for Each of Us

Jacob knew the depth of his other sons' hatred toward Joseph but still harbored a hope for family harmony. When the brothers were to go north to Shechem, to find better grazing for the sheep, and remain there for several weeks, Jacob seized the chance to effect a reconciliation between the dreamer and his hostile siblings. Jacob thought that if only they could spend time together away from home, where Joseph was seen as the preferred son, they could be reconciled. If he had merely wanted to see how his sons and the flocks were faring in Shechem, Jacob would have sent one of his servants. Sending a seventeen year old alone on the journey from Hebron, in the south, was quite perilous and only made sense if there was some ulterior motive. The motive was simple for Jacob: Just as he had to confront his brother Esau at the Jabbok in order to overcome the distance between them, so, too, Joseph had to be strong enough to confront his brothers on his own if there ever was to be unity in the family.

When Jacob called Joseph, telling him his brothers were herding the sheep near Shechem and that he wanted him to go and see how they were doing, Joseph became utterly frightened. He was smart enough to realize that, away from his father's protection, his brothers would have him exactly where they wanted him—alone and vulnerable. Yet, somehow he mustered up enough courage to respond: *"Hineini,"* I am ready to go. Like his ancestors before him, he uttered

still harbored...
Genesis 37:11 indicates that "Joseph's brothers hated him, but his father kept (*shamar*) the matter in mind."

go north to Shechem...
Genesis 37:12.

telling him his...
Genesis 37:13–14.

[155]

the one word which indicated that he had no choice but to respond positively when someone he loved requested he act on their behalf. The task was fraught with obvious danger. He knew what awaited him in the fields of Shechem. Nevertheless, he could not say no to his father, the only person who truly cared for him.[9] Our ability to respond often does depend upon who is calling us. If it is someone we respect or love, our parent, spouse or child, we often have no choice but to say: *Hineini.* We have to respond to them, and in so doing, reciprocate their love for us.

When he said *hineini* to his father, Joseph thought he was simply to visit his brothers and report back to Jacob. At most he expected to be gone for a few days. Little did he know, however, that the next time he would see his father's face would be twenty-seven years later in Egypt. The next time he would see his father, Jacob would be very old and nearing the end of his life. There was even a real possibility that he would never see his father again. The chance to say *hineini,* to respond to the father whom he loved so much, may never have come again. In addition, his trip to Shechem did not merely involve visiting his brothers, but was the beginning of a four-hundred-year journey of slavery and redemption for the Jewish people.

Our lives are no different than Joseph's. The limited task we accept is often not the task that we actually complete. Our simple actions can have a more significant impact than we could ever envision. When we do an errand for an aging parent, spend some time with our child or merely have a kind word for someone we encounter, our actions are an important part of *tikkun olam,* the repair of our world. Simple acts of every individual are crucial if we want not only to improve the important relationships in our lives, but also to make this world a better place.

tell a story about... B.T. *Sanhedrin* 98a.

The rabbis tell a story about R. Joshua ben Levi who, when walking near the cave of R. Shimon bar Yohai in Safed, met the prophet Elijah. Knowing that he was the herald of the messiah, he asked Elijah when the messiah would come. Elijah responded by saying that he should ask the messiah himself, who could be found sitting among the poor at the gate of the city. What a magnificent metaphor. In order to discern the messianic, to see the potential for the redemptive in the world, we have to look at the faces of the poor and stare into their eyes. By responding to the poor in our midst, we can help foster the repair of our world. So when a friend of mine always places food that she takes home after dinners out in the container of a homeless man who is camped out on her corner, she, like R. Joshua ben Levi, plays an important part in *tikkun olam*.

We also should cherish the opportunities we have to respond to those who mean so much to us. We may never have those chances again. I think of a day two years ago just before Passover when I was sitting in my office in Manhattan. The phone rang and I heard the voice on the other end say: "Hello, Normyboy." I knew immediately that my father, calling from Houston where he was visiting my brother for the holiday, wanted something from me. He asked me to go out to his apartment an hour away in Queens, and check to see if he had secured all the locks and emptied the mailbox before he left for Houston. I told him that I did not have a lot of time and I couldn't get there, but assured him that he indeed had closed the police lock, the chain and the door bar. He asked again and I begged off, saying that I would do it the following day. As life would have it, the very next morning the telephone rang, but this time it was my brother Marvin calling to tell me that Pop had died moments before. I sat holding the phone and crying. I couldn't help but think about the previous morning's conversation. I wished I had said to him, "Sure Pop, I'll go out to Astoria if it's important to you." The phone doesn't ring anymore with the voice calling "Normyboy." I would love to hear it one more time, so I could replay the last conversation with Pop. Chances to say *"hineini"* do not last forever; we never know when they will be gone. If only we had the wisdom to use them to the best of our ability.

Joseph Searches for His Brothers: We All Need to Find Our Other Side

Joseph did respond to his father and set out to find his brothers. That Joseph had difficulty locating them in Shechem underscores that the purpose of his journey had more to do with the nature of their relationship than simply seeing how their shepherding was coming. He had to find and repair his relationship with his brothers before he could move on with his life.

he realized he was lost... Genesis 37:15

Joseph was approaching Shechem when he realized he was lost.[10] He searched in vain for his brothers' camp, and he had almost given up hope of finding them when he lifted up his eyes and saw a man on the road walking toward him. At first he was afraid since he could not make out the stranger's features. His mind flashed back to a story his father had told him about a similar encounter he had many years ago with a strange man near the Jabbok before he was reunited with his brother Esau. He recalled how Jacob literally shaking when he recounted wrestling with the stranger until dawn broke, and how the limp he had was the result of the battle. His father also said the struggle with the man had prepared him for the moment when he saw Esau again. If he could survive the battle with the powerful, almost god-like stranger,[11] then he knew he surely could find the strength to confront his own flesh and blood. As these memories flooded his head, Joseph became even more afraid of the man who appeared larger as he approached. Perhaps he, too, had to overcome this stranger, this apparition on the road, before he could find his brothers.

But when the stranger came closer, Joseph saw his slight smile and heard him asking something, though he was not sure of the exact words. Joseph thought he had said, "What are you searching for,"[12] so simply answered, "It is my brothers whom I desire."[13] With these words, Joseph began to cry silently. He, indeed, needed and felt absolutely lost without them. He pleaded with the stranger to tell him if he knew where his brothers had pastured their flocks.

Joseph thought he said... Genesis 37:15–16.

The man responded that the brothers had departed. He had overheard them say they would set up camp near Dothan. This seemed strange since the fields were more lush in the area around Shechem than further north. Joseph conjured up all sorts of scenarios, chief among them that his brothers heard he was coming and had left to avoid seeing him.[14] Just when he wanted to be reconciled with them, they were running away from him. He had no choice but to follow and headed north to Dothan.

the brothers had departed... Genesis 37:17.

Taking Revenge on the Dreamer: Our Resentment Can Lead to Violence

Though Joseph found his brothers in Dothan, the reunion did not turn out as he and his father hoped. From the moment they spotted him in the distance, even before he had a chance to draw near and explain how he felt, his siblings conspired against Joseph. Their anger was so great and their resentment of his dreams so deep they had only one thought—to kill him.

they spotted him... Genesis 37:18.

But then the unexpected happened. Reuben spoke up in an attempt to save Joseph's life. The firstborn son, who had so disappointed his father when he defiled his bed by sleeping with Bilhah, wanted to prove that for once he could act responsibly on his father's behalf. In so doing, he would be reconciled with Jacob and maintain the birthright. Reuben did not know at this point that his actions would be

when he defiled... Genesis 35:22.

Reuben saved his...
Genesis 37:21–22.

to no avail, since eventually he would lose his primary position in the family to Joseph. Reuben saved his brother's life by suggesting the brothers not kill him but simply toss him into an open pit in the wilderness. All the while he intended to return surreptitiously, draw Joseph out of the pit and bring him back to their father. Reuben's actions reflect a real ambivalence on his part, and perhaps on the part of all the brothers. After all, Joseph was their flesh and blood. They may have been fond of him, though at the same time angered by his arrogance and visions. The pit, which became Joseph's refuge and saved his life, symbolizes this ambivalence.

When he approached...
Genesis 37:23–25.

When he approached, the brothers ripped off Joseph's ornamented cloak, the very object that signalled his favored position, and threw him into an empty pit. Although they did not shed his blood, if left there he would surely die of thirst and starvation. And then the brothers immediately sat down near the pit to eat a meal, underscoring how as a group they were set against him. While he languished in the dry, empty pit, the brothers broke bread together. We are left wondering how Joseph felt in his isolation. Did he call out to them, pleading for his life, only to have his cries fall on deaf ears as they sat and leisurely partook of the food they had prepared? Could the chasm between Joseph and his brothers ever be overcome? However, one brother was missing. Reuben had left the group and returned to the pit to save Joseph's life.

Before this could happen, Judah spotted a caravan of traders approaching from a distance and took advantage of the opportunity to speak up. Judah clearly was the strongest personality. He dominated most conversations. He was also the most respected, the one everyone looked to for leadership, including Jacob. There was little affection and respect for Reuben, especially since the Bilhah episode, which his brothers understood as an attempt to usurp his father's

attempt to usurp...
See Bereshit Rabbah(NV), Chapter 97 in this regard.

[160]

power. Judah was in a position to save Joseph's life. The brothers would surely listen to him.

Therefore, when Judah urged them to sell Joseph to the oncoming caravan that was moving slowly on the road south to Egypt, carrying gum, balm and laudanum, they immediately agreed. He convinced them they could not take the life of their own flesh and blood.

caravan that was...
Genesis 37:26–27.

Judah indeed saved Joseph's life. Yet, by convincing the brothers to sell him into slavery, they became guilty of a capital offense. It was tantamount to killing him! But why didn't Judah do more? Could he not easily have persuaded them to return Joseph to their father? Judah had the opportunity to act in a heroic manner by doing the right thing but fell short. More than all the other brothers, Judah bore a guilt that would haunt him in the months ahead.

Judah bore a guilt...
Midrash Tanhuma Buber *Va-Yeshev* #8, 12, Shemot Rabbah 42:3 and Midrash Sekhel Tov 38:1.

Judah pays the price of being recognized as a leader in the family. He is not unlike those of us who are older brothers or sisters, who frequently feel a special responsibility to insure that all is right with the members of our family. Some of us may have carried that burden with us since we were children, and to this day, we still are anguished when enmity and strife are present among our siblings, or between any one of them and our parents. By contrast, our brothers or sisters may seem to be able to live more easily with family disharmony and rancor.

Judah Distances Himself from His Brothers: Strife Often Leads to Fragmentation in Our Families

Joseph survived the desert journey with the caravan and was sold to Potiphar, a member of Pharaoh's court. Once ensconced in Potiphar's house, Joseph was oblivious to everything that transpired back in Canaan. He knew, however, his father would be distraught when he discovered that he, Joseph, was gone. And he correctly imagined that his brothers would concoct an outlandish story to explain what had happened. Indeed they told their father they had nothing do with Joseph's disappearance; some kind of wild animal had devoured him. As proof, they insensitively asked their father to examine Joseph's multicolored tunic, which they had dipped in the blood of a slaughtered kid. The brothers not only did away with Joseph, but they also destroyed their father as they had killed the animal. Jacob mourned for his son, whom he now knew was dead, and refused to be comforted. He felt his life was over and wailed that he was going to go down to Sheol to be with his son.

father to examine...
Genesis 37:31ff.

Jacob mourned for...
Genesis 37:34–35.

The pain the brothers' actions caused their father was enormous; they regretted what they had done. And in their remorse, led by Reuben, they began to point fingers at Judah as the one most responsible. After all, it was his plan they had listened to and followed. If Judah had not pushed them in the wrong direction, they would have changed their minds and released Joseph. To scare him would have been enough, was the claim now advanced.

they regretted what they...
Genesis 37:38.

Castigated by his brothers for not meeting the responsibility he bore, Judah distanced himself from them. It was almost as if he had been banished from their midst. Judah's separation is indicated by the words, "At that time, Judah left (*va-yeired* literally means "went down from") his brothers." *Va-yeired* tells us much about Judah's moral condition.

Judah distanced himself...
Genesis 38:1. See Bereshit Rabbah 85:1.

While Joseph was being brought down to Egypt, Judah went down from Beer Sheva to the camp of his friend Hirah, the Adullamite. Both of Jacob's sons were separated from their brothers. And as their stories develop, both are objects of seduction—Judah by his daughter-in-law, and Joseph by Potiphar's wife. The stories of Judah and Joseph were quite directly linked. The linkage is solidified by the use of the verb *yarad* (went down) in both.

The linkage was solidified...
In Genesis 39:1 Joseph is "brought down to Egypt." See also Bereshit Rabbah 88:2 and Yalqut Shimoni 1, *remez* 144.

[162]

Judah Lies to Tamar:
It Is Too Easy to Justify Our Unethical Actions

As the story of what happens to Judah develops, we learn that after falling in love with and marrying Hirah's daughter, he fathers three sons, Er, Onan, and finally Shelah who was born at Cheziv. When they later recalled his birth, it must have appeared most ironic to both Judah and Bat Shuah that they named him Shelah, which means "mislead," and that he was born at Cheziv, the place of deception. If only they had known ahead of time the significance of the name and place in the larger scheme of things. The names help the reader anticipate the deception on Judah's part which is about to occur.

In time, Judah found a wife for his firstborn son, Er, a Canaanite woman named Tamar, whose lineage is not known.

a wife for his...
Genesis 38:6.

But when Er was killed by God for acting in an evil manner, Judah gave his next son, Onan, to her, thus fulfilling the obligation of the brother to insure the continuity of his deceased brother's line. However, Onan refused to stand in his brother's stead, and chose to spill his seed so as not to provide him with an offspring. When God took Onan's life as well, Judah feared for his remaining young son, Shelah. Although he was obliged to give Shelah to Tamar, he counseled her to live in her father's house until Shelah came of age, implying that he then would fulfill his responsibility to her. He never intended to do so. Shelah would not die like his brothers, even if Judah had to deceive his daughter-in-law. This was not the first time Judah had not lived up to what was expected of him. His previous actions caused Jacob to lose a son; now that he himself had already lost two sons, he was not about to lose his youngest.

Judah gave his...
Genesis 38:7–10. This is called Levirate marriage. See Deuteronomy 25:5 in this regard.

And it is clear that Judah was convinced he was right. At least he had convinced himself of the justice of what he had done, since he gave little thought to Tamar from that day forward. It is so easy to shirk responsibility when we can rationalize our actions. We know the pattern well. Think of all the times we have told untruths or have not fulfilled promises we made in the name of higher values, all the time knowing in our heart of hearts that we've done something wrong. In most cases, these involve minor issues and we call them excuses or stories. Yet, they can create a pattern of behavior that leads to greater lies and deceits. In Judah's case, he deceived Tamar and in the process lost himself. Ironically, a short time later, Judah's own wife died. He, like Tamar and Jacob before him, suffered a terrible loss, though unlike his daughter-in-law and his father,[15] who would never get over their losses, Judah went through the period of mourning and was comforted. The hurt he had inflicted upon others was lasting; he, on the other hand, rose up from his mourning and went up to Timnah to join his friend Hirah and the other men for sheepshearing.[16] While he went off to sow his oats, what he would uncover on the road to Timnah was very close to home.

though unlike his daughter...
Genesis 38:12.

the period of mourning...
Genesis 38:13.

The Opening of Judah's Eyes: Seeing Ourselves for What We Are?

harlot sitting at the...
Genesis 38:14.

"Judah went up...
Genesis 38:12.

Judah would face his true self, in the guise of a harlot sitting at the entrance to the village of Einaiyim.[17] Judah's eyes were opened and he began to recognize who he was and what he had done. The text says that "Judah went up (*va-ya'al*) to Timnah." The verb *alah* stands in tension with *yarad* (go down) used before to describe Judah's leaving his brothers, his descent from them. His rise to his higher self was about to begin.[18]

Hearing that Judah was coming up to Timnah, Tamar became infuriated. She was not able to get on with her life, but her father-in-law could pick himself up after Bat Shua's death and start all over again. This was not fair or right. She realized that Judah was never going to fulfill his obligation to her; she never would marry Shelah. Tamar was bent upon showing him just what kind of a man he was. With all of his power, he might not have to recognize her just claims. But he would get to know her and come to understand of what she was made.

So she took off her widow's garb, put a veil over her face and sat down at the entrance to Einayim, where the harlots congregated. As she sat there waiting for Judah to appear on the road, she thought to herself that she indeed saw the truth, and Judah was about to see it too.[19]

sat down at the...
Genesis 38:14.

Are we not all like Judah? We think of ourselves as being bright, introspective, and honest. Yet, often we deceive ourselves into thinking that our less-than-altruistic acts are surely justified and we would never hurt anybody. It may take an encounter with someone—someone from whom we don't expect to learn much—to open our eyes and help us see clearly, perhaps for the first time.

I remember riding on the subway several months ago and, feeling very tired, I rushed to take the only vacant seat in the car. I was oblivious to everyone around me. It was only when a young construction worker tapped me on the shoulder and berated me for not giving the seat to an elderly gentleman standing nearby that I realized what I had done. I am sure that I've acted in the same way before, especially on my trip home at the end of the day when it is so easy to feel that the empty seat is just waiting for me. It took a laborer in a dirty tee-shirt and jeans to open my eyes. Indeed, a Canaanite harlot sitting on the road to Timnah can bring us to our own *Petah Einayim,* the opening of our eyes.

that Judah saw...
Genesis 38:15–16. In contrast to Tamar who recognized Judah for what he was, he did not know her.

All that Judah saw immediately was a mere harlot, sitting at the crossroads, her accustomed place; so he turned aside and sought to engage her. When she asked how much

When she asked...
Genesis 38:17.

inquired about the pledge...
Genesis 38:18.

Tamar informed him...
Genesis 38:24–25.

"Recognize please if this...
Genesis 37:32.
See also Midrash ha-Gadol to Genesis 38:1.

he was willing to pay, he replied he would send her a young kid from his flock.[20] She demanded a pledge, to insure he would keep his promise (Tamar knew Judah had difficulty keeping promises!). And when Judah inquired about the pledge, the *aravon,* Tamar demanded nothing less than his seal, cord and staff. Her request struck Judah, and he gasped. How could she demand these items, the very symbols of his status; the signs of his tribal standing. He did not understand that she was entitled to his family status in the first place. Though unable to share this before, at Timnah in a moment of passion, Judah gave in to his desires. He gave little thought to the significance of his seal, cord and staff. And Judah and his daughter-in-law Tamar slept together. Unknowingly he had taken the place of Shelah, fulfilling the obligation of providing his deceased sons with heirs.[21]

Almost miraculously, Tamar conceived and in her womb carried twins. Tamar had forced Judah to perform the levirate duties of the youngest brother, and at the same time fulfill his responsibilities as a father. Tamar had to teach Judah that the lost brother must be redeemed, something he had not understood as he stood over Joseph in the pit.

Three months later, it became obvious to all that Tamar was pregnant. Judah, informed that her condition was the result of harlotry, ordered her killed. However, Tamar informed him, saying: "I am with child by the man to whom these belong," and added: "Recognize please to whom this seal, cord, and staff belong." As Judah listened to her voice, quiet yet strong with resolve, his mind flashed back to the words he had spoken to his own father when showing him Joseph's coat dipped in the blood of the kid: "Recognize please if this is your son's tunic." The words sounded strangely the same: *Haker na ha-hotemet,* and *Haker na ha-kutonet,* as if one was the retribution for the other.

Judah was forced finally to recognize the injustice of his actions and the pain he had caused both Jacob and Tamar.

As he stared at the seal, cord and staff, and saw that they were his, the emblems of who he was or at least ought to be, at that moment he took an honest look at himself.[22] He was forced to struggle with his other side, the shadow that was always there, but which he had never confronted. And as he did, he said for all to hear: "She is more righteous than I, inasmuch as I did not give my son Shelah to her."

"She is more... Genesis 38:26.

Tamar Teaches Judah Who He Is: We All Must Learn Who We Are

For Judah, as it is for every one of us, this brief moment of honest reflection, struggle and then recognition of what he had done was the first step toward his return to his brothers and to his higher self. Indeed it was a major reason why he deserved to have the messianic line of David emanate from him.

it was a major... See the Mekhilta d'Rabbi Ishmael, *Beshallah, parashah* 6 and its many parallels.

While Judah is its progenitor, however, the Davidic line is traced through one of the twin sons born to Tamar. For like Rebeccah before her, Tamar gave birth to twins, Perez and Zerah, who struggled to see who would emerge from their mother's womb first. While she was in labor, one of the infants, Zerah, put forth his hand and the midwife tied a crimson thread around his wrist to signify that he appeared first.[23] However, his twin burst forth ahead of him, and so he was named Perez, the one who made a breach. As it had been with Isaac and Ishmael, and Jacob and Esau, Perez, the younger of the two, would stand in the line leading to the messiah.

the Davidic line... Ruth 4: 18–22.

Judah, the major force in selling Joseph into slavery and the father who had refused to meet his responsibility to his daughter-in-law, a Canaanite of inconsequential lineage, was the one from whom the Davidic line emerged.

How powerful it is to consider that it was the son Tamar bore, Perez, who continued that line. Like Ruth, her

stands in the Davidic...
Again see Ruth 4:20, where Ruth's son Oved, through Boaz, is the grandfather of King David.

Moabite counterpart whose progeny also stands in the Davidic line, she was a non-Israelite. Yet, through her actions, she played a major role in guaranteeing the survival of the nation of Israel. Righteousness is not the product of family status or societal position, but rather of the actions of individual human beings regardless of their backgrounds.

Each one of us can move the world closer to the messianic. Tamar teaches Judah, and through him, all of us, what it is to be a member of God's people. Often it is the stranger in our midst who teaches us what God expects of us. The one whose heart is directed purely to the Holy One, whose life is a demonstration of spiritual commitment, serves as a mirror for me and for you, who at times take our heritage for granted. Tamar models what we are and what we are capable of becoming. Not only is she a key to the change in Judah and to the role he would play in the developing story of Joseph and his brothers, but it is her righteous actions which we confront every day.

Joseph in Potiphar's House and in Prison: Leaving Home Is Often the Beginning of Our Growth

From the moment Judah took the lead and suggested that his brothers sell Joseph to the Ishmaelite traders and not have his blood on their hands, he became their spokeperson. He assumes the dominant role in the ongoing narrative, and symbolizes all the other brothers as he stands over against Joseph. The tension between the two of them is the axis around which the rest of the story turns.

taken down to Egypt and...
Genesis 39:1.

The saga of the brothers continues with Joseph taken down to Egypt and sold to Potiphar,[24] whose wife soon tried to seduce him. But unlike Judah who succumbed to Tamar on the road to Timnah, Joseph refuses the persistent advances of his master's wife. We begin to see a maturing Joseph who takes seriously the responsibility placed upon him to run Potiphar's household. He also invokes God's name for the first time, when he says: "How then can I do this most wicked thing and sin before God?" The egotistical dreamer who knows only of his own desires has begun to fade. We begin to see a more serious, ethical Joseph developing.

Joseph's growth began when he left his father's protective presence and set out on his own. Away from the oppressive attitude of his brothers and their jealousy, he could begin to look at himself in realistic terms. It often takes leaving their parents' house for children to begin to develop a stronger sense of themselves and take responsibility for their lives. How many of us have been utterly amazed at the transformation of our kids when they go off to college. It almost seems that overnight they became serious about things which had little significance for them all the years they were at home. Caring for their clothes, being responsible for chores, and taking assignments seriously are the more superficial issues—they also seem to care more genuinely for others and as they become less moody and self-absorbed, they are actually a pleasure to be with for more than a few minutes.

As if to emphasize the important connection of this event to Joseph's past, as well as to indicate how he had already changed, we learn that one day, when no one else was in the house, Potiphar's wife grabbed his outer garment and pulled him towards her. As she implored him to lie with her, he pulled away leaving her holding his coat, and fled. As he was running from Potiphar's house, the vision of his brothers tearing off the multi-colored coat which his father had given him flashed before his eyes. It seemed like only yesterday, though much time had passed. The feelings of vulnerability which he now experienced were similar to those he had felt then.[25] Yet, he surely was different. In ripping off his coat, his brothers had unmasked him; they had shown

He also invokes God's...
Genesis 39:7–9.

his brothers tearing...
Genesis 39:11–12. See in this regard Genesis 37:23, which also refers to Joseph's outer garment.

just how ridiculous were his dreams and his illusions of importance and power. Now, as he spurned the advances of his master's wife, he no longer needed a facade to cover his true nature. Potiphar's wife had encountered a special young man. And her subsequent claim that Joseph's intent was "to make fun of [her household]" could not be further from the truth. He may have enjoyed taunting and chiding his brothers before. Now he simply acted responsibly.

intent was "to make fun...
Genesis 39:14,17.

Even though his motivations were pure, symbolically Joseph was cast back into the pit from which he had been delivered to Egypt and Potiphar's house. Hearing the accusations of his wife, Potiphar became furious with Joseph and put him in prison. All the time Joseph spent in prison, he thought he was back in the pit into which he had been thrown by his brothers. And he even referred to the prison as "a pit" with resonances of his prior experience. For when pleading with the chief cupbearer to mention him to Pharaoh when the cupbearer was released from prison, Joseph said in a most telling way: "I was kidnapped from the land of the Hebrews; nor have I done anything here that they should have put me in a pit." Joseph's three years in prison paralleled the three days he languished in the pit in Dothan.

Hearing the...
Genesis 39:19–20.

"I was kidnapped...
Genesis 40:15.

Before, Joseph was thrown into the pit by his brothers because of his dreams of grandeur. This time, Joseph's stay in "the pit" would end because of his ability to interpret the dreams of others. When the Pharaoh dreamed of seven cows by the Nile and seven ears of grain, the cupbearer remembered how Joseph had correctly interpreted his dreams in prison and mentioned it to Pharaoh. Pharaoh then ordered that Joseph be removed from the dungeon/pit, dressed handsomely, and brought before him. During his three-year stay in prison Joseph had continued to mature. Like his brother Judah, he struggled with his true nature and his other side. The Joseph who dreamed of the sun, moon and stars bow-

When the Pharaoh dreamed...
Genesis 41:1–13.

ing down to him and his brothers' sheaves of wheat bowing down to his sheaf was disappearing. We now encounter a more empathetic Joseph who is able to interpret the dreams of others, all the while acknowledging God's help. The haughty youngster is no more; a kinder, more humble Joseph is emerging. The dreamer now becomes the vehicle of interpretation, God's mouthpiece. As a result, he is released from the pit and begins his meteoric rise to power in Egypt.

When Joseph begins to show real humility, as he reminds Pharaoh that God is the power in the universe and that God will see to his welfare, Pharaoh appoints Joseph as his viceroy, saying: "Since God has made so much known to you, there is no one more discerning and wise than you. You shall be in charge of my court....I will put you in charge of all the land of Egypt." Joseph rises from the pit to sit at the righthand of the Egyptian throne; the very same Joseph, the spoiled dreamer, who was ostracized by his brothers and carried down to Egypt by a caravan of Ishmaelite traders.

that God is the power... Genesis 41:16.

"Since God has made... Genesis 41:39–41.

The Meeting of Joseph and His Brothers: Taking the First Step toward Reconciliation

As Joseph became more and more immersed in his life in exile, taking an Egyptian name given to him by the Pharaoh, marrying Asenath, the daughter of Poti-phera, the priest of On, and emerging as the chief authority in Egypt next to Pharaoh, memories of his family and Canaan grew dim. So much so that when he became the father of two sons, he named his firstborn son Manasseh, meaning, "God has made me forget completely my hardship and my father's house." Joseph was now an Egyptian through and through, and he no longer was haunted by dreams of being abandoned by his brothers nor of his journey to Egypt on the slave caravan which had stayed with him for years.

marrying Asenath... Genesis 41:45.

"God has made me... Genesis 41:51.

Yet, as fate would have it, his brothers too would sojourn

Jacob heard that food...
Genesis 42:1–2.
We would have expected the text to describe them as "Jacob's sons."

his brothers must have...
Bereshit Rabbah 91:2, Targum Yerushalmi to Genesis 42:6 and Midrash Tanhuma ha-Nidpas, *Miketz* #8.

There was even some...
Sefer ha-Yashar 30:24.

the vizier of the land...
Genesis 42:6.

in Egypt and be reunited with him. For when a famine struck, Jacob heard that food rations were to be had in Egypt and sent his grown sons, ten in number, down to Egypt to purchase grain. With the exception of Benjamin, all Joseph's brothers went to Egypt. The emphasis on the fact that it was his (as well as Benjamin's) ten brothers who set out for Egypt only serves to underscore their impending confrontation. The ten brothers, including Judah, were as one arrayed against Joseph. The two sides of the family—the progeny of Rachel and Leah—were about to meet and the struggle between brothers continue.

Yet, their meeting offered the possibility of a rapprochement. For surely on the long trek with the pack animals, his brothers must have spoken of Joseph, wondering what had happened to him since they saw the traders whisk him off to Egypt. As they recalled what had occurred in Dothan and the ensuing pain it caused their father, they must have felt deep regret at what they had done. He, after all was still their brother and each time they looked upon Benjamin, Rachel's other child, they were reminded of their sinfulness. There was even some talk of trying to locate Joseph in order to ransom him. And if his master refused, some of the brothers, led by Reuben and Judah, vowed to fight if necessary. However, they were also anxious about seeing him again. How would he react? Would he hate them and refuse to talk to them? Perhaps he would refuse to return home with them.

When his brothers arrived in Egypt, they were told that if they wanted to purchase grain, they had to come before Zaphenath-Paneach, the vizier of the land who was in charge of dispensing rations. The powerful man before whom they found themselves was none other than their younger brother Joseph, who had once dreamed of lording his power over them. As if in fulfillment of his youthful dreams, the brothers bowed low with their faces to the ground. When he finally glanced their way, he was astonished to recognize them *(va-yakiraim)*, though they had no notion of who he was *(va-yitnaker)*. It was not only his position and accoutrements that fooled them, but the changes wrought over the years of separation in both his physical presence and his persona. And he acted like a stranger to them, as they had to him when they plotted to kill him. It was his turn to do the plotting, though it is not clear what his intention was at this point.[26]

He spoke harshly, asking whence they had come, all the time wondering why they had ventured down to Egypt. Had they changed, perhaps, and come to Egypt in order to find him and undo the harm they had done? Had the years changed them and what was their makeup now? He remembered them as they were when they cast him into the pit; but were they the same persons now standing before him?

The brothers still had no clue as to the Egyptian official's identity. Nevertheless, standing before Joseph, they underscored their familial connection by stressing that they were all sons of the same man![27] And as if to emphasize even further that he was a part of them, they added that they were twelve brothers, the youngest of whom was with their father while one was no more. The tension is clear: Though the brothers are torn apart, they remain connected. They will always be sons of the same father, even though they are separated from the children of Rachel. The brothers constitute two sides of one whole.

Like Joseph, we, too, may be distanced from one or more of our siblings, yet we continue to struggle with them and what they represent for us. We can truly never totally excise them from our hearts and minds; we carry them with us wherever we go like an old suitcase bearing mementos from our past. Only when we come face to face with them again will we be able to discard the baggage with which we have been burdened.

he recognized them...
Genesis 42:7.

stressing that they...
Genesis 42:11.

they added that they...
Genesis 42:13.

The Brothers Imprisoned in Egypt:
Things Have a Way of Coming Full-Cycle

He placed them all...
Genesis 42:17.

one of them must remain...
Genesis 42:19–20.

They cried out that...
Genesis 42:21–25.

now one of them...
The parallelism between Joseph and Shimon is mentioned in several places, including Tanhuma ha-Nidpas, *Va-Yiggash* 4.

It is not surprising then that almost everything that happened to Joseph in Canaan because of his brothers' ill-treatment, now is visited upon them when they come before the powerful vizier of Egypt. The tables have turned. Joseph is presented with the very same options his brothers had when they stood over him in the pit. He easily could have killed them in revenge, but chose a different path: He placed them all in the guardhouse, claiming that they might be spies. Like Joseph in the pit in Dothan,[28] they spent three days uncertain of their fate, only to learn that one of them must remain in detention while the others returned to Canaan in order to bring Benjamin down to Egypt. Just as Joseph had been terrified to remain alone in the pit for what seemed an eternity, one of them now would experience the same fate.

The fact that they are made to suffer the same circumstances and treatment is made absolutely clear when the brothers themselves perceive that they were being punished because of what they did. They cried out that they were suffering on account of their brother Joseph. Reuben was even more explicit: "Did I not tell you, 'Do no wrong to the boy?' But you paid no heed. Now comes the reckoning for his blood!" Not only would Joseph and his brothers—the two sides of the family—undergo the exact same hardship, but they themselves were responsible for it in both cases.

But there is more. For after they sat in the guardhouse for three days, Joseph took Shimon, had him bound and remanded to prison as a guarantee that the others would fetch their youngest brother from their home in Canaan and return to Egypt. Just as Joseph was isolated by them, now one of them would experience the identical fate. Shimon was cast into the pit while his siblings journeyed home from Egypt.

[174]

When the brothers arrived without him, their father Jacob was quick to draw the parallel, saying: "It is always me whom you bereave; Joseph is no more and Shimon is no more, and now you would take away Benjamin....My son must not go down with you, for his brother is dead and he alone is left. If he meets with disaster on the journey you are taking, you will send my white head down to Sheol in grief."

"It is always me... Genesis 42:36.

The repetition of events which occurred some twenty-two years before becomes even clearer as the story develops with Benjamin as the focus. For just as Jacob had announced that he would go down to Sheol mourning the loss of his beloved Joseph, now he reiterates that the loss of Benjamin would have the same effect. Joseph and Benjamin, the progeny of Rachel, are clearly seen as one by their father, and elicit from him the same feelings and reaction. Benjamin is the embodiment of Joseph in his father's eyes.

Jacob announced that he... Genesis 37:35 and 42:38.

Promising to Protect Benjamin: Acting upon Our Potential to Change

Although the events that surround Benjamin's journey to Egypt surely echo the sale of his brother Joseph into slavery, there are from the outset hints that this time the outcome will be different. Whereas none of the brothers really put himself on the line to save Joseph, and all in some way were involved in getting rid of him, this was not so in the case of his younger brother. First Reuben assures Jacob that if he places Benjamin in his care, he will guarantee his safe return. He even goes so far as to say to his father: "You may kill both of my sons if I do not bring him back to you." Just as Jacob would lose a second son, now Reuben was willing to sacrifice his two sons.

"You may kill... Genesis 42:37.

Later, when the famine became severe, and the family is in desperate need of more food rations from Egypt, it is obvious that if they were to return to Egypt, Benjamin would have to accompany them. Judah speaks up, promising to care for Benjamin and take responsibility for his life. "I myself will be the surety for him," he pledges to Jacob, "and if I do not bring him back to you, I shall stand guilty before you forever." The very same Judah who had not been willing to fight for Joseph; Judah who had not been willing to fulfill his responsibility to Tamar, but who was willing to give her a pledge in order to lie with her, now becomes the pledge![29] He will guarantee Benjamin's life.

"I myself will be...
Genesis 43:9.

The Brothers Admit Their Guilt:
The Beginning of Our Integration

Whatever would be the outcome of the promises of Reuben and Judah, the journey down to Egypt with their youngest sibling must have called to mind the sale of Joseph to the Ishmaelite caravan. From the very moment they told their father Joseph's demand that Benjamin be brought back with them, their own words seem to indicate what they felt. When Jacob pressed Judah as to why he told Joseph about Benjamin, he explained that Joseph kept asking about the family and inquired whether they had another brother.

he explained that Joseph...
Genesis 43:7.

Of course, Joseph's question applied equally to himself as well as his younger brother Benjamin. And when he told the brothers to bring Benjamin down to Egypt, just as he was "brought down to Egypt" by the Ishmaelite traders, the symmetry of the story is sealed. The brothers who were responsible for Joseph being brought to Egypt, would now actually carry Benjamin down to Egypt themselves. In addition, when their father at first refused to allow Benjamin to leave, claiming it would end his life, they could not help but recall the special affection and concern Jacob had exhibited for Joseph. They were again forced to face the fact that both these sons of his old age, whom Rachel had born, were the special objects of his love. They must have been jealous of Benjamin, as they were of Joseph before him. Just as they had the opportunity to attack Joseph at Dothan, when he was removed from his father's house, now Benjamin would be under their power during the long journey to Egypt. One had to wonder whether they even would treat him kindly. Whatever was to happen, Benjamin was now following in his older brother's footsteps, as he, too, was part of a caravan loaded with spices heading south.[30]

Not only did the brothers carry spices and nuts with them, but Jacob gave them double the money to give Joseph as restitution for the money inadvertantly brought back from Egypt in their saddle bags. Their hope was that Joseph would release Shimon and leave Benjamin unharmed. The brothers who sold Joseph into slavery for twenty pieces of silver, now would exchange the money not only to secure the release of their brother Shimon, but to guarantee young Benjamin's safety. And Joseph, who was sold into slavery, would now receive money from those who sold him. Unknowingly, the first step towards reconciliation already had been taken. Seeing Benjamin after the caravan arrived in Egypt not only brought Joseph to tears, but even closer to revealing himself to his brothers. This was indeed his mother's son, his closest kin. In many ways, Benjamin was like his son, an extension of himself, and he treated him accordingly, when he received the family in his palace.

However, when his brothers were leaving, Joseph had his servants place his silver goblet in Benjamin's saddle bag, along with the alloted rations. He even had to laugh at the idea. Could there be a better choice of object for the false accusation against Benjamin than his silver divining goblet that recalled the silver for which he had been sold? On the one hand, it served as a reminder of his brothers' brutal act toward him and their attendant guilt.[31] He even went so far as to instruct his steward to tell his brothers, when he had

part of a caravan...
Genesis 43:12.

Jacob gave them...
Genesis 43:12,21.

Seeing Benjamin after...
Genesis 43:29–34. Joseph actually refers to Benjamin as *"beni,"* my son.

that it was an evil...
Genesis 44:5.

overtaken them in order to bring them back, that it was an evil thing for them to do. The remark raised the spectre of Dothan. But the silver goblet was also the vehicle by which Joseph would discern if indeed they had changed. Would they turn on Benjamin and desert him, as they had done to him? Confronted by the challenge that the one in whose bag the goblet was found would become Joseph's slave while the others could go free, what would they do?

in whose bag...
Genesis 44:5.

Upon the discovery of the goblet in Benjamin's possession, the brothers rent their clothes, demonstrating the pain they truly felt. Benjamin's siblings, the same ones who ripped the coat off Joseph and caused their father Jacob to rend his garments in mourning over the loss of his son, now appear before Joseph in tattered garments. Yet, at the same time they are moving towards a greater sense of themselves.

in mourning over the loss...
Genesis 44:13 as well as 37:23 and 34.

Precisely at this point the brothers collectively admit their guilt. Judah, speaking for the others, says to his brother Joseph: "What can we say to my lord? How can we plead? How can we prove our innocence? God has uncovered the sin of your servants." Although they indirectly admit Benjamin's guilt, they seem to indicate that they share the responsibility. It was God's will that they be punished because of their real crime—selling Joseph into slavery. They bear the actual guilt and not the one in whose saddle bag the goblet was found. But Joseph pushes the issue; he wants to repeat the scene: He insists that Benjamin remain alone in Egypt as his slave, while the brothers return in peace to Canaan. Benjamin, the extension of Joseph, will suffer as he did.

"What can we say...
Genesis 44:16. See also G. Plaut's comment on the verse in his *Torah Commentary*.

that Benjamin remain alone...
Genesis 44:17.

Once again unsurprisingly Judah takes the lead in arguing for Benjamin's life. After all, of all of Joseph's brothers, only Judah seems to be as forceful as Joseph. When Joseph insists that Benjamin remain with him, Judah steps forward as the spokesperson for his brothers. He seems ready to do battle with the viceroy of Egypt.

The dialectic involved in Judah's confronting Joseph is based on a play on the word *va-yiggash* (Judah approached). The root *nagash* can also imply conflict.

Judah's confronting... Genesis 44:18. See also Bereshit Rabbah 93:2 and Bereshit Rabbati to Gen. 44:18.

Although he speaks in a rather delicate and supplicating manner, the forceful intent of his words is clear. In fact, one could get the impression that Judah would not have taken no for an answer; he was willing to fight if necessary to free Benjamin and return him to their father.

he was willing to fight... Midrash Tanhuma ha-Nidpas Va-Yiggash #5 and Bereshit Rabbati to Genesis 42:7.

Perhaps Judah's plea to Joseph, which focuses on his father's relationship with Benjamin and the grief it would cause him if Benjamin remained in Egypt, reveals the reason why Judah was willing to put himself on the line for Rachel's youngest son and Joseph's full brother. His description of Benjamin as the child of Jacob's old age upon whom he dotes and how Jacob would die if anything happened to Benjamin could as easily have been said about Joseph himself.

His description... Genesis 44:30–31. See also Bereshit Rabbah 93:8.

The more Judah went on about Jacob's love for Benjamin and how he should not be taken from his father, the more he underscored his own guilt and that of his brothers in relation to Joseph. This reaches a crescendo when Judah finally adds that he has sworn to his father Jacob that if he does not return Benjamin to him, he will stand guilty forever. Only in saving Benjamin's life can he expiate his deep guilt for what they did to Joseph. Leah's sons must now repent for their past sins.

adds that he has sworn... Genesis 44:32.

The Moment of Truth—
Can People Truly Change?

Do we believe that we human beings have the capacity to grow in substantial ways over time, especially knowing ourselves as we do? Or is our attempt at change simply a matter of making small adjustments to personalities and patterns that are fairly well fixed? Do we know in our hearts that our essential makeup remains unaltered or can we become better?

Perhaps Judah (and the rest of Joseph's brothers) can serve as an affirmation of and a paradigm for our own ability to change. Perhaps as Judah stood before Joseph as Benjamin's advocate, he consciously recalled the fateful day years before at Dothan. Then he was given the chance to save his brother Joseph's life and return him to his father, but instead took the easier way out by uttering the words, "Let us sell him to the Ishmaelites and be done with him." Joseph languished in the pit for three days and Judah never was moved to intervene on his behalf. Now, in a replay of that scene, when Benjamin is about to be incarcerated, Judah is given another opportunity to fulfill his responsibility. This is the moment of truth for Judah. Would he act differently than in the past? Had he changed at all? This is a classic example of the rabbinic notion of *Teshuvah* (Repentance)— to be in the same place under the same circumstances in which we sinned and now act differently.

Standing before Joseph, Judah demonstrates the potential each of us has to grow and mature. In great humility, he reminds Joseph that he has pledged himself to his father to insure the boy's safety and he pleads with Joseph to allow him to take Benjamin's place as Joseph's servant.[32] With much emotion, he adds that he cannot witness the pain it would cause his father if Benjamin did not return. No such sentiment was present when Judah and his siblings showed the blood-stained coat of his son Joseph to Jacob and forced him to think Joseph had been killed by a wild animal. How cruel they were when they uttered the words: "Examine [the coat] and see if it is your son's tunic or not?" and how callous Judah and the brothers were as they stood by witnessing their father rending his garments in mourning and bewailing the loss of his young son. Yet, now Judah is willing to sacrifice himself for Benjamin, the younger sibling of

"Let us sell..."
Genesis 37:27.

that he has pledged...
Genesis 44:32–33.

that very Joseph. The brothers had changed and the potential for reconciliation was present.

Joseph too seems to have changed radically. From the moment he was confronted by his brothers at Dothan and thrown into the pit, he maintained a distance from his family. If there is anything that characterizes Joseph in the long saga it is his silence in the face of his brothers' hostility.[33] This was his means of protecting himself. However, it not only was an expression of his determination to endure and survive, but of his desire to cut himself off. The chasm was enormous and at times appeared unbridgeable.

Are our relationships with our siblings any different than the relationship of Joseph and his brothers? How many of us feel that the rift between us and our brother or sister is so wide that it can never be healed? As I mentioned before, my own father and uncle had a severe falling out and they did not speak to one another for ten years, and there were many times that my father indicated that he felt that they never would get back together. So much time had passed and so much anger had developed that the distance between them seemed to him insurmountable.

Yet, at the moment when Judah approached and uttered words of love and concern for Benjamin, Joseph could no longer hide himself from them. Revealing his identity, he burst into loud sobbing. In turn his brothers were silent, dumbfounded by his revelation. As he beckoned them to come closer, they were overwhelmed to hear him say the words: "I am your brother Joseph." Their brother was still alive and he was assuring them that he held no ill will toward them. He emphasized that his coming to Egypt was part of God's plan to save their lives in the famine. They were struck by his words of forgiveness and his invitation to the entire family to dwell near him in Egypt so that he could care for them. Although addressing his words to his father Jacob, the brothers heard Joseph's words personally; each

"I am your brother...
Genesis 45:2–4.

was part of God's...
Genesis 45:4–8.

"Come down to me...
Genesis 45:10–11.

Esau fell upon...
Genesis 33:4.

embraced his brother Benjamin...
Genesis 45:14–15. Many of the same verbs are used in the encounter between Jacob and Esau.

felt he was talking to him: "Come down to me without delay....You will dwell in...Goshen, where you will be close to me....and there I will provide for you."[34]

And just as Esau fell upon the neck of Jacob, embracing and weeping with him at the moment of their encounter near Mahanaim, so now Joseph embraced his brother Benjamin around the neck and kissed his other siblings and wept with them. Like Esau, Joseph initiated the reconciliation and only then could his brothers summon the strength to speak to him. The same brothers who slandered him to their father and could not speak a friendly word to him, now shared words of love and affection. They, indeed, had finally come close to one another again; the sons of Rachel and the sons of Leah were united as they never had been before. And unlike Jacob and Esau before them, who though they were able to meet and establish some relationship, were unable to remain together, Jacob's sons were truly reunited.

The Blessing of Ephraim and Manassah: Our Two Sides Can Come Together

Most startling is the fact that only in their coming to Egypt were Jacob's children united together as a family. And they are the first family in the Book of Genesis to remain together.[35]

The unity of Jacob's family and the rapprochement between Joseph and his brothers is evident in the manner in which the numbers of the family who went down to Egypt are counted. After enumerating all of Jacob's sons and their wives and children, which added up to a total of sixty-six, Joseph, his wife and his two sons, Ephraim and Manasseh, who were born in Egypt, are included, thereby bringing the number to seventy in all. Joseph and his sons are an integral part of Jacob's family.

Sometime after settling in Goshen, Jacob became ill and

enumerating all of Jacob's...
Genesis 46:26–27.

Joseph, realizing that his father might soon die, brought his two sons to him for his blessing. Joseph wanted to make sure that Ephraim and Mannaseh would be included in the covenantal promise that belonged to Jacob's progeny. And as he stood in front of his father, clutching the arms of his two boys who were born in Egypt to an Egyptian mother, he saw his father place his sons on his knees and heard his father say: "Now your two sons shall be mine; Ephraim and Manasseh shall be mine no less than Reuben and Shimon." Jacob had made Joseph's two sons his own.[36] He placed them on his knees *(birkav)* and blessed them (Jacob gave them his *berakhah*), and in so doing, bridged the chasm between the children of Rachel and Leah forever. Joseph began to cry as he saw his aged and almost blind father reach out and grab hold of his two boys, pulling them close to him. Joseph could not help but remember the story his father told him of the day when his grandfather Isaac blessed him instead of his uncle Esau. Isaac, too, was almost blind when he passed on the covenantal blessing to Jacob, as Joseph hoped Jacob would to his sons. As his father kissed and embraced each of them, just as he had kissed and embraced his own brother Esau many years before,[37] Joseph finally felt that he had come home. The family was together again, and the wounds of the past were behind them. Joseph believed that no longer would siblings fight over the birthright; no longer would the younger son take away the blessing intended for the older.

So Joseph eagerly removed his sons from his father's lap and placed them in front of him to receive a blessing; he set Manasseh to his father's right, as he was the firstborn, and Ephraim to his left. Joseph was astonished when his father stretched forth his right hand and placed it on Ephraim's head, though he was the younger, and put his left hand on Manasseh. Joseph objected strenuously as his father crossed his hands.[38] "Did he simply make a foolish mistake," Joseph

"Now your two sons...
Genesis 48:5, 12.

father reach out...
Genesis 48:10.

as his father crossed...
Genesis 48:13–14.

thought to himself, "or was the change intentional?" But when Joseph tried to switch his father's hands, Jacob insisted that although Manasseh would be the progenitor of a great tribe, Ephraim, the younger son, would surely achieve greatness.

Joseph tried to switch...
Genesis 48:17–18.

Joseph was angry that his father seemed to perpetuate the very rivalry between the siblings he himself experienced with his brother Esau. Once again, it seemed that the younger was to supplant and receive the blessing intended for the older. Jacob's confused blessing of Joseph's sons was also a duplication of his own experience in his father's house, as well as that of his grandfather, Abraham. The tension and strife seem to continue. Yet, Joseph's concerns were mollified when he realized that his father was going to bless Ephraim and Manasseh together, and actually heard his father utter the words: "By you shall Israel invoke blessings, saying: God shall make you like Ephraim and Manasseh." Although Ephraim's name was mentioned first, both were blessed at the very same time with the very same words. Neither one was exalted over the other; they were to share only one blessing and they no longer would have to wrestle with each other.[39] And what is more, every time children in the future receive a blessing from their parents, it will be given in the name of Joseph's sons. They, too, will be blessed like Ephraim and Mannaseh; they too, will stand together facing the future as equals. The two sides had come together and occasioned God's blessing now as well as in the future.

"By you shall...
Genesis 48:20.

If the people as a whole were to survive, then the rejection of one part had to end. Like each and every family, and like each one of us individually, coming to wholeness demands that we accept each part of ourselves and our family in order to achieve some degree of unity. The struggle had to end somewhere and it stopped with Jacob's sons, all twelve of whom remained a part of the people and shared in its destiny.

[184]

And so when Jacob was about to die, he gathered his sons together to tell them what the future held in store. Before he addressed each one of them, he warned against any dissention and urged them to understand that their future as a people depended upon unity.[40] Their survival and ultimate redemption was dependent upon the oneness they would achieve.

he addressed...
Genesis 49:1.

He then proceeded to bless each of his sons individually. Each one received a blessing; no one of them was given an exclusive blessing as such. All therefore had a share of the blessing that had been handed down from Abraham through his son Isaac to their father Jacob. Even though the blessings are not the same, nevertheless, they all shared in the legacy of the past and in their people's destiny. No two individuals are alike; each has a unique potential.

Yet, it was not surprising to any of the brothers that special blessings were given to Judah and Joseph. From the earliest days, Judah and Joseph were the focus of much of what transpired in the family and were seen by their father as the most important sons. Therefore, it made sense that they would represent the keys to the family's future. Jacob pictured Judah as a lion, strong, courageous and ruler over all. And the scepter and the staff (the same staff that Judah had given away to Tamar), the symbols of power and authority, would never pass from him as the ruler. No wonder that subsequently stories began to circulate among the tribes that Jacob had even predicted that the messiah would eventually come from the tribe of Judah![41]

Jacob pictured Judah...
Genesis 49:9–10.

Although Joseph and Judah were utterly different, Jacob made it clear that their futures would be intertwined. Though it was Joseph who dreamed that his brothers would someday bow down to him as they did, Jacob here portrays them bowing low to Judah. Similarly, when their father described Judah's garments washed in wine and his robe in the blood of grapes, they could not help but think of their

Jacob here portrays...
Genesis 49:8 and a parallel in 49:24.

garments washed in...
Genesis 49:11.

Joseph, still his father's...
Genesis 49:23–26.

as a mighty warrior...
Genesis 49:27.
The same verb *taraf* is used in connection with both Benjamin and Judah.

dipping Joseph's coat in the kid's blood in order to fool their father.

Authority and power might not come to Joseph, nor would he be the progenitor of the messianic. Yet, Joseph, still his father's favorite, would receive an abundance of wealth from God. Like Judah, his tribe would be powerful warriors who would defeat their foes, and they would be truly blessed. Joseph would receive his father's greatest material blessings, far surpassing those which even Jacob himself received; the blessings of heaven and earth. Joseph, though not to hold the mantle of rulership like Judah, would be seen as the elect of his brothers. Whatever Judah's glory, Joseph was to be set apart from his siblings.

Benjamin, too, was described by his father as a mighty warrior. Like his brother Joseph, but even more like Judah, he would prey on his enemies. Just as the blessings of Joseph and Judah have much in common, Benjamin, the other part of Rachel's progeny, and Judah are linked. Indeed, the futures of their tribes are tied together. The tribes of Judah and Benjamin, the southern tribes of Judea, together will represent the continuity of the nation when the northern tribes are defeated and exiled. Judea, whence the Jewish people emanate, was to be made up of descendants of both Leah and Rachel—of Judah and of Joseph's brother and extension, Benjamin.

The battle was over. Jacob as the patriarch of Israel lived to see his family united and his sons gathered together in harmony. The tension that characterized the previous generations, beginning in the Garden of Eden and moving through Adam's sons, Abraham and his family, the generation of Isaac's children, Jacob and Esau, and Jacob's struggles in Laban's house together with Leah and Rachel, dissipated. The wholeness that had been missing since the days of creation seems to have been achieved. The sides have finally come together. And even though after Jacob's death the brothers feared that Joseph would kill them, just as Esau had planned revenge on his brother Jacob once their father Isaac would no longer be alive, Joseph, who had changed, eased their fears. He assured them that he held no grudges toward them and he guaranteed that he would sustain them.

after Jacob's death the... Genesis 50:15 and 27:41.

The very same Joseph who had tattled on them, speaking harshly about them to their father, now could speak only kindly to them. The same Joseph who expected his entire family to worship him, bowing down in homage and recognizing his power, now is able to admit that he is not God and there was absolutely no reason for his brothers to fear him.[42]

eased their fears... Genesis 50:19–21.

is able to admit... Genesis 50:19f.

Joseph himself had grown and achieved a degree of harmony and peace. His family in turn had come together as never before. They would live together in Egypt and his brothers' descendants would carry his remains back with them to their ancestral homeland.

| ▮ |

THE TWO MESSIAHS:

When the Different Sides Come Together

Life is a search for meaning. We seek ourselves as we strive to understand our complex natures. Through our struggle with others—our parents, children, and siblings—and most of all through our internal struggle with the other side of ourselves, we change. But just how much? Are we able to come to grips with our darker side, the shadow of our personalities, and at the same time recognize and reach towards our highest selves? Can we achieve real wholeness and holiness in our lives?

The conflict between siblings and their inner struggles pervades the entire Book of Genesis. From the moment of the creation of humankind in the Garden of Eden as an androgynous being made up of two parts, the fabric of the biblical narrative is woven from tales of conflict and tension. Perhaps the end of Genesis can only be written when the equality of Ephraim and Manasseh and the peaceful relationship between the descendants of Rachel and Leah are achieved. Only then can Judah and Benjamin, the two remaining tribes that make up the southern kingdom of Judea, representing the future of the Jewish people, be joined forever.

Just as Genesis closes with the unity of the people of Israel, we, too, may see the day when we will experience peace within ourselves and with the significant others in our lives. But when will that day come?

And is the struggle over even for our biblical forebears? As we move into the Book of Exodus and embark upon the journey of the the tribes toward the promised land, do the two sides indeed become unified? Or does the tension and struggle of the journey, through the heat and aridity of the desert, indicate that the harmony of which we dream in our lives has not yet been fulfilled for Jacob's heirs? The trek through the desert is a metaphor for our own life journey through the prosaicness of every day, in which we search for poetic moments of song, for water, for a resting place and for God's mountain. The time in the wilderness speaks to us of our continuing struggle, conflict, pain and change.

The Ephraimites Leave Egypt Too Early: Sometimes We Seek Change Too Eagerly

At times, though we want to change, we are simply not ready, and no matter how hard we try or what we do, nothing seems to work. This even was evident with the Israelites at the outset of their journey to the land of Canaan. As the tribes were preparing to flee Egypt and the oppression of four hundred years of slavery, conflict arose among them. For after the tenth plague, prior to God's command for the people to flee under the cover of darkness, the Tribe of Ephraim thought the time of redemption had arrived and left without waiting for their brothers and sisters. Because

conflict arose among them... The Mekhilta d'Rabbi Ishmael, *Shirta, parashah* 9, B.T. *Sanhedrin* 92b and Shemot Rabbah 13:17.

they left before the appointed time, the story circulated that their defeat by the Philistines was divine punishment.

But when the story was told of the battle of the Ephraimites with the Philistines, much respect and honor was accorded to the members of this powerful Joseph tribe. Theirs was simply a tactical mistake; they had miscalculated the timing of the moment of redemption, the result of their burning desire for the nation to be free.[1] The legend circulated among the people over the generations that because the tribe of Ephraim erred in calculating the time destined for redemption and were killed by the Philistines, God would not be comforted until the blood of the Ephraimites was avenged.

So, when the Israelites encountered the Amalekites in the wilderness, it was appropriate that Joshua, the son of Nun, an Ephraimite and the grandson of Joseph, would lead the tribes into battle and carry them to victory. The people believed that Moses knew that only a descendant of Rachel could conquer the descendants of Esau. Joshua thus avenged in part the blood of his kin through the Israelites' desert victory. And the people came to believe that the dead of Ephraim whose bones lay scattered in the wilderness would live again. Centuries later when the prophet Ezekiel (6th century B.C.E.) spoke of the dry bones coming to life, his vision was believed to be that of the Ephraimites who died at the hands of the Philistines. Like the phoenix, they would rise out of the fiery flames.

A similar story about an ill-timed flight from Egypt circulated about a second Rachel tribe—the tribe of Benjamin. It was told that when the tribes stood facing the waters of the Red Sea, with the Egyptians in hot pursuit, the tribe of Benjamin jumped in first. But the heads of the tribe of Judah began to stone them, insisting that they had miscalculated the moment when God wanted them to enter the water in order to effect the redemption. However, the tradition

Because they left.. This notion is based perhaps on Psalm 78:8–10 and on 1 Chronicles 7:20ff.

much respect and honor.. B.T.*Sanhedrin* 92b.

Ephraim erred in... Shemot Rabbah 20:11.

Amelekites in the wilderness... Exodus 17:13. See also Bereshit Rabbah 75:12.

a descendant of Rachel... Bereshit Rabbah 99:2 and Exodus Rabbah 26:3.

that of the Philistines... See, for example, the Targum Yonatan to Exodus 13:17.

A similar story... Mekhilta d'Rabbi Ishmael, *Beshallah, parashah* 6.

emphasizes that both tribes were to be rewarded, since they showed their faith in God's redeeming powers. Though the Benjaminites misjudged the time when God expected them to act, the Temple would be erected in their territory, while the messianic line would emanate from the tribe of Judah.

Even during the desert journey of redemption we see that the tension between the children of Rachel and Leah, the struggle between the progeny of Joseph and Benjamin on the one hand, and that of Judah on the other, continues. The two sides still vie for power and leadership, and the people are still fragmented. Yet, the respective roles they will play must be seen as a part of the collective dreams of the people together for freedom, wholeness, and peace. If the messianic vision of the Jewish people is ultimately to be realized, it is clear that the descendants of both Joseph and Judah will have an important part. Both parts of Jacob's family are indispensable if the people of Israel is to fulfill its destiny as a nation covenanted with God.

Likewise each of us will come to greater wholeness only if the disparate parts of ourselves and our families can join together. Through the recognition of who we are and the importance of the different sides of our makeup, we can begin to build towards a higher vision of ourselves. And then by acting upon that vision, we can help hasten the coming of the messianic age. As we have emphasized, seemingly simple, mundane acts—responding to a poor person on the street or finding the strength to say *"hineini"* to those for whom we care—as well as working for peace and justice wherever we can, are all a part of *tikkun olam,* the repair of our world.

The Two Messiahs:
Change and Ultimate Wholeness Will Be Ours

The stories about the premature exodus of the tribe of

Ephraim from Egypt led to the belief in the advent of a first messiah, the son of Joseph (Ephraim), a military figure who will precede the coming of the second messiah, the son of David. Just as the leaders of the tribe of Ephraim attempted to bring redemption through military actions prior to the appearance of the son of David, so will it be at the End of Days. The wars of the first messiah, the son of Joseph, will precede and indicate the coming of the scion of David.[2]

Probably influenced by the prophecies of Zechariah (late 6th century B.C.E.), who refers to two annointed ones, several messianic figures are mentioned as early as the Dead Sea Scrolls as being counterparts to the messiah, the son of David.[3] Early on, however, the second messiah, described as a military figure, came to be identified with the tribe of Ephraim.

Later, eschatological traditions emphasized that prior to the advent of the true messiah, the world would experience a series of catastrophes, "messianic birth-pangs," a kind of Armageddon. The world was pictured as suffering labor pains prior to the coming of the Messiah, the son of David. At this time the heroic messianic warrior, the son of Joseph, would appear to lead the Jewish people. He, however, would fall in battle, to be mourned by the whole house of Israel.[4] Only then would the Davidic Messiah, the descendant of Judah, appear and defeat the forces of darkness without resorting to conventional means of warfare. In this way the time of ultimate peace for Israel and for all humanity would be ushered in.

The struggle between the descendants of Leah and those of Rachel, between the two sides of Jacob's family, the two sides of each and every one of us, seems to be eternal. The messiah, the son of Joseph and a leader annointed for war, would have to fall in battle before the true messiah, the scion of David and Judah, could emerge. Perhaps like his Ephraimite predecessors who left Egypt too soon, his ac-

prophecies of Zechariah...
Zechariah 4:14.

identified with the tribe...
See, for example, the Targum to Shir ha-Shirim 4:5 and 7:2, as well as Bereshit Rabbah 95, Bamidbar Rabbah 14:1 and Targum Yonatan to Exodus 40:11.

messianic birth-pangs...
In Hebrew, *Hevlei ha-Mashiah.* See B.T. Sanhedrin 97a-98b.

would appear to lead...
B.T. *Sukkah* 51b-52b.

tions were destined to fail.

Yet, this is not how the apocalyptic drama concludes. Just when we expect the struggle between two messianic figures to end with one of them dying to make way for the predestined leader of the people, God's annointed one, we find the opposite. The rabbis' messianic vision is not one of eternal tension and competition between two foes. Rather there is a final coming together of the two seemingly disparate forces into a unified whole. Israel is pictured as going up to Jerusalem, led by Elijah and the Messiah, the son of David. There, amidst the peals of the shofar's blast, the fallen Messiah, the son of Joseph, will be resurrected, ushering in the messianic age. The revived Messiah of Joseph will then be sent to gather in the exiles from the four corners of the earth. In the end, he is portrayed as sitting in the honored position at the side of the true Messiah, the son of David, the one who rules the world through enduring peace.[5]

True unity and wholeness is possible. While all of us individually, and collectively as a people, are destined to struggle with the different sides of ourselves, with our siblings and with the divine in us, the ultimate union of Judah and Joseph provides us with a model and strengthens our hopes. Such was the vision of the prophet Ezekiel:

vision of the prophet...
Ezekiel 37:15–22.

The word of the Lord came to me: "And you, O mortal, take a stick and write on it, 'Of Judah and the Israelites associated with him'; and take another stick and write on it, 'Of Joseph—the stick of Ephraim—and all the House of Israel with him.' Bring them close to each other, so that they become one stick, joined together in your hand....and you shall declare to them: Thus says the Lord God: 'I am going to take the Israelite people from among the nations...and gather them from every quarter and bring them to their own land. I will make a single nation in the land, on the hills of Israel, and one ruler shall rule over them. Never again shall they be two nations, and never again shall they be divided into two kingdoms.'"

If only each of us would believe that Joseph and Judah can come together as one, that families and relationships can be repaired and that individuals can find healing. Then change will take place. The biblical promise will be fulfilled. The prophets constantly held up that vision for us, and the rabbis accentuated it. Isaiah pictured the wolf and the lamb grazing together, and the lion eating straw like the ox. Indeed, no matter how long the lion of Judah and the ox, who is Joseph, struggle as enemies, in the End of Days they shall sit together and share their food in peace.

the rabbis accentuated... Bereshit Rabbah 95:1 and Bereshit Rabbati to Genesis 46:28.

We, like our primordial ancestor Adam, were divided in two at the moment of our creation and are destined to spend our entire lives struggling with the other side of ourselves. And like Adam and Eve who ate from the Tree of Knowledge, and were expelled from the Garden of Eden, we journey through the seasons of our lives in search of our higher selves, trying to find the divine that is present in each of us. And we long to return to God's place—to the Garden. Like Cain before us, we search for our lost sibling and like Jacob and Esau, and Leah and Rachel, we continue to struggle with our brother or sister in the hopes of someday drawing closer, of really coming together again. As the progeny of Jacob, the tribes of the northern and southern kingdoms, we long to be joined again one to another, and recreate the wholeness we had at the beginning.

Isaiah pictured... Isaiah 65:25.

This we can experience in our lives if only we would find the courage to open ourselves to the sacred stories of our past and imbibe their power and meaning. Through our involvement in the text, we will discover ourselves in the process.

May it be God's will that our immersion in the holy words of Torah may help us to reach that day and speed its coming.

| | |

Introduction

1. Mel Gussow's review, "Sam Shepard Revisits the American Heartland," in the *New York Times*, December 15, 1985, p. 22.
2. See Claude Levi-Straus, "The Structural Study of Myth," *Journal of American Folklore* 68 (1955): 428–441 in this regard.
3. Stephen Crites, "The Narrative Quality of Experience," *Journal of the American Academy of Religion* 39 (1981): 304.
4. Wolfgang Iser, *The Act of Reading* (Baltimore: Johns Hopkins Press, 1978), p. 22ff.
5. Robert Alter, *The Art of Biblical Narrative* (New York: Basic Books, 1981), p. 114.
6. See a number of stories in *Ancient Near Eastern Texts*, ed. James Pritchard (Princeton, N.J.: Princeton University Press, 1955).
7. See, for example, "The Contest of Horus and Seth for the Rule" in *Ancient Near Eastern Texts*, pp. 14–17. Yin and Yang in Chinese thought are perceived to be two contrary yet complementary forces.
8. Carl Jung refers to these tendencies as "shadows." See his *Collected Works* (Princeton N.J.: Princeton University Press, 1969), Vol. 9: 8–9; 11: 76–78, 197–98; and 14: 497.
9. Alter, *The Art of Biblical Narrative*, p. 176 and Arthur Waskow, *Godwrestling* (New York: Schocken Books, 1978), pp. 10–11.
10. J.P. Fokkelman, *Narrative Art in Genesis* (Amsterdam: Van Gorcum, 1975), pp. 3–4.

Chapter One

1. Scholars understand this second story to have emanated from a different literary source than the one found in Chapter One.
2. By contrast, the spelling with one *yod* in verse 19, in which the creation of the animals is described, is more regular.
3. Eric Silver, "Tarnished Angel," *The Jerusalem Report* (December 30, 1993), p. 43. The title prompted the use of the

term below.

4. The question is magnified by the phrase which follows, since the subject vacillates between the plural and singular: *"They* said: *I* will sing to the Lord."
5. Philo's *Questions and Answers on Genesis and Exodus*, #25 to Genesis 2:21.
6. See in this regard Phyllis Tribble, "Depatriarchalizing in Biblical Interpretation," *Journal of the American Academy of Religion* 41 (1973), p. 37.
7. This is emphasized in the play on the phrase, *"tov me'od,"* which is taken to mean *"tov adam"* (man is good) by transposing the letters. See Bereshit Rabbah 9:12.
8. See Arthur Waskow's comments in *Godwrestling*, pp. 48–50.
9. This is further reflected in the fact that the word *tzeila* has the additional meaning of "misfortune" or "lameness."
10. In his work *Godwrestling*, p. 50, Arthur Waskow stresses that "Goodness cannot be naive,...[but] we must struggle with evil in order to do what is truly good."

Chapter Two

1. This is underscored when, in contrast to our opening verse, he is referred to by his proper name at the end of the chapter (4:25).
2. References to the Tree of Knowledge aside, the biblical writer could have chosen other words to describe their sexual encounter; but he chose to use the verb "to know."
3. We have here the the explanation of Cain's name. He is called *"Kayin"* in Hebrew because Eve says, *"kaniti"* (I have gained).
4. This notion reflects the obvious misogynous view of the Ancient Near East as well as of the rabbis.
5. One of the best known epithets for God is *"koneh ha-kol,"* the creator of everything. Eve, too, felt that she was a *"koneh"*.
6. The point is based on the word association of *bechorot* (firstlings) and *bachar* (chose).
7. John Steinbeck, *East of Eden* (New York: Penguin Books, 1986).
8. The word used in the text is *sha'ah*, which literally means that God did not turn towards him, or look closely at him and his offering.
9. The verb in Hebrew, *taitiv* (do well), is future tense and, therefore, God's challenge to Cain should be understood in

this manner.

10. See Elie Wiesel, *Messengers of God* (New York: Random House, 1976), p. 63.
11. Some early traditions do indicate that Cain said to his brother,"Come, let us go out to the field." For example, the Samaritan Bible, the Septuagint and the Peshitta.
12. Wiesel, *Messengers*, p. 56f.
13. This is underscored by the play in v. 4 between *Hevel* (Abel) and *helev* (fat). Abel himself became the preferred offering.
14. We see that Eve experiences pain for both of her sons, as she did in childbirth.
15. The underlying play is on the verse: *"Ha-shomer achi anochi"*—God (Anochi) is my brother's keeper!
16. The word for silence in Hebrew is *demamah,* which is quite close in sound to *dam,* meaning blood. It is almost as if the text says, "The silent voice of Abel cries out."
17. When the verb *arr* is used with the preposition *min,* it means "to hold off" or "to ban." See E. Speiser, *The Anchor Bible, Genesis* (New York: Doubleday, 1964), p. 24, n. 14.
18. See also Wiesel, *Messengers*, p. 43.
19. This understanding of the phrase is consonant with the translators' negative predisposition to the fratricidal murderer.
20. Many of the early Bible translations understand *mi-neso* as "to be forgiven." Perhaps the word *neso* has some resonance with the word *seyt* in v. 7.
21. The words are from Psalm 92:1, which is ascribed in the Tradition to Adam. The term *lehodot,* which means "to praise," is interpreted here as "to confess."
22. Three things are referred to as an *ot,* a sign of covenant: The rainbow following the flood, circumcision, and the Sabbath. All three possess redemptive implications.
23. The mark of Cain also reflects other biblical references to protective marks (placed upon the forehead) which were intended to show that the bearer belongs to the Deity.
24. *Kedem,* east, seems to be a symbol of banishment. Devora Steinmetz, *From Father to Son: Kinship, Conflict and Continuity in Genesis* (Louisville: John Knox Press, 1991), pp. 90–91.
25. See Arthur Waskow's insightful comments on what we can learn from the story in his *Godwrestling,* pp. 17–21.

Chapter Three

1. Nahor's absence is stressed further by the family settling in a place called Haran. Haran had died sometime before, but he was symbolically still with them.
2. The text says: "Thus they parted *(va-yippardu)*, the one from his brother." The same verb is used in Genesis 25:23 to describe the break between Jacob and Esau.
3. See in this regard the comments of D. Steinmetz, *From Father to Son*, p. 92.
4. The wordplay in Hebrew is wonderful: Sarah says that she "will be built up" *(ibaneh)* through Hagar by the birthing of a son *(ben)*.
5. This point is stressed also by the rabbis. See, for example, Bereshit Rabbah 45:3.
6. See p. 89.
7. The dialogue shifts back and forth in Genesis 17 between a focus on one son or the other, stressing the relationship and the tension between them.
8. The redundancy in the text underscores the contrast between Isaac and Ishmael: "Abraham gave his new-born son, whom Sarah had born him, the name of Isaac" (Genesis 21:3).
9. However, Arthur Waskow suggests that Isaac's laugh was one of joyous triumph, while Ishmael's was filled with hurt and rejection. See his "The Cloudy Mirror: Ishmael and Isaac," *CCAR Journal* (Autumn, 1977), p.21.
10. The rabbis suggest that the term *metzahhek* means that Sarah became irate over Ishmael's treatment of Isaac. See Bereshit Rabbah 53:11.
11. *The New Yorker,* February 28, l994, p. 62.
12. The rabbis emphasize the parallelism between the two life-threatening tests by labelling the banishment of Ishmael and the binding of Isaac as Abraham's ninth and tenth trials.
13. See some interesting comments in this regard by Marc Gellman, "After These Things," *Masoret* (Fall, 1991), pp. 10–11.
14. The twelve tribes of Ishmael are enumerated in Genesis 25:12–16 paralleling the listing of Jacob's twelve sons in Genesis 35:22–26.
15. Rashi describes Abraham's *hineini* as the language of humility, the willingness to limit oneself in recognition of "the other"

and the demands made.

16. It seems that following God's creation of Adam and Eve, the Divine provided all that they needed to survive outside the Garden of Eden.

17. Perhaps we have here a play on the literal meaning of the phrase, *"ayil ahar."* The term *ahar* could mean "behind," thereby telling us that the ram was behind Abraham. The rabbis also play on the phrase *"ne'echaz b'karnov."* Although the simple meaning is that the ram was "caught...by its horns," the word *karnov* is taken to mean "its corners."

18. This recreation is based upon a portion of an anonymous prose piece in Hebrew from Israel, which was translated into English over thirty years ago by Rabbi Wolli Kaelter.

19. The word *yachdav* is used twice previously in describing how Isaac accompanied his father on the journey to the mountain (Genesis 22:6,8)—they had indeed proceded *together.*

20. Abraham's loss of his sons is underscored by the recounting of his brother's large family in the next paragraph (Genesis 22:20–24).

21. Since Sarah's death follows on the heels of the *Akedah,* the rabbis see a causal relationship between the two events. See, for example, *Sefer ha-Yashar,* Genesis 22.

22. The biblical text even tells us later that Isaac did in fact settle down there (Genesis 25:11).

23. In chapter 25:11-12, the emphasis on Isaac dwelling in *Be'er lahai roi* is followed by mention of Ishmael: "And Isaac settled near *Be'er lahai roi.* This is the line of Ishmael...."

24. Isaac and Ishmael might have been reunited at *Be'er lahai roi.* Note the rapprochement between them as pictured by the rabbis in the Book of Jubilees 2:1–3.

25. Isaac is even pictured as mourning for Ishmael for many days when he died. See *Sefer ha-Yashar* 29:19 and *Midrash Aggadah* to Genesis 25:5.

Chapter Four

1. Her pain is emphasized by the play on the Hebrew *be-kirbah* (inside of her) which inverted reads *be-Rivkah* (inside Rebekkah).

2. The Hebrew term used to describe Jacob and Esau struggling is quite emphatic—*va-yitrozzu,* from the root *rzz,* meaning "to tear apart, to shatter."

3. It is said that "[Rebekkah] went to inquire of the Lord,"

probably meaning that she consulted an oracle.

4. The word *yipparedu* clearly breaks up a pattern in the Hebrew of four phrases of three beats each. It sticks out and as such seems to be key.

5. Jacob, the *tam,* and his brother, Esau, are viewed as parts of a larger whole (the plural, *tomim,* twins). See Bereshit Rabbah 58:8 and Midrash Lekah Tov to Genesis 25:23.

6. See, in this regard, the contrastive descriptions of Gilgamesh, the king of Erek, and Enkidu, a wild and hairy savage in *The Epic of Gilgamesh,* Tablet 1, Col. 2, line 36.

7. *Akav* does mean "to follow at the heel of," but it can also mean "to deceive." Jacob not only steals the birthright, but he will deceive his father in Chapter 27.

8. See Alter, *The Art of Biblical Narrative,* p. 43.

9. In Hebrew, Esau is called a *yodeia tzayid,* matching Isaac's taste for game *(tzayid).*

10. Wiesel, *Messengers of God,* p. 112.

11. After losing his blessing, Esau marries Mahalat, Ishmael's daughter. The rabbis fill in the dialogue between uncle and nephew in Sefer ha-Yashar 67:8 and Midrash ha-Gadol to Genesis 28:9.

12. The text actually uses the word *aiyef,* which usually is translated as tired, and not famished. Genesis 25:29, 30.

13. For example, when Isaac, on the road to Mt. Moriah, calls to his father, saying *"avi,"* my father, Abraham responds, *"hineini veni,"* here I am, my son.

14. Jacob selects two choice kids from the flock and tricks his father by wearing the animals' skins. This anticipates his own sons dipping Joseph's tunic in the kid's blood to feign his death (Genesis 37:31–33).

15. See David Fass, "Unbinding Mother Rebekkah," *Judaism* (Fall, 1992), p. 374.

16. Even the rabbis recognize this duality. See, for example, Midrash Sekhel Tov to Genesis 27:23.

17. The term for guile, *mirmah,* is the very word that Jacob uses in Genesis 29:25 to describe how Laban will fool him. See p. 132.

18. See Maurice Samuel, *Certain People of the Book* (New York: Alfred A. Knopf, 1955), pp. 158-159.

19. We can only speculate how Esau and his mother might have related to each other during the twenty years in which Jacob

dwelt in Haran.

20. Fokkelman, *Narrative Art in Genesis*, pp. 203–204, focuses upon Jacob's use of the word *"katonti"* (unworthy), meaning, "I am small," as a sign of his willingness to assume the role of the younger son.

21. The thrust of the rabbinic tradition is that Jacob struggled with Esau's protective angel, his guardian.

22. The root of the word for wrestling used here is *avak,* which literally means dust or dirt. It is also very similar in sound to the name Ya'akov and to Yabbok.

23. The so-called "sacred touch" should have been decisive, but it did not have the predicted effect. See Fokkelman, *Narrative Art in Genesis,* p. 214.

24. Fokkelman, *Narrative Art,* p. 203.

25. Note the possible play in the Hebrew between *"tuchal,"* meaning "prevail," and *tachil,* meaning "to include," or "integrate."

26. They tore each other apart in the womb—it said *va-yitrozzu,* from the verb *rzz* (Genesis 25:22). Now Esau ran towards Jacob *(va-yaroz),* from the similar verb *rz.*

27. The soundplay between the roots *avak* (struggle or wrestle) and here *habak* (embrace) also emphasizes the shift from conflict to reconciliation.

28. The ambiguity of meaning of such phrases as *va-yippol al tzavarav* (he fell on his neck) highlights the tension between the two sides and at the same time, the potential for harmonizing them.

29. Fokkelman, *Narrative Art,* p. 225.

30. The word play between *mahaneh* (camp), *hen* (favor) and *minhah* (gift) stresses that it is possible to reach beyond the defensive camp to reestablish relationship.

31. Jacob actually uses the word *kappar* (atone) when he instructs his servants, "If I propitiate *(akhapara)* [Esau] with presents, perhaps he will show me favor" (Genesis 32:21).

32. Esau accepted Jacob *(va-tirzeni).* The root *rzh* is similar to *rzz* (struggle) and *rz* (run) which were used before. The movement is from struggle and conflict, to running towards each other, to acceptance.

33. The term *neged,* however, can mean "near," but it also means "opposite" or "against." Thus the text hints at the continuing tension between the brothers.

34. If the term is meant to convey the meaning of "peacefully" or

"in peace," we would expect the text to read *"b'shalom."*

35. The description of the separation of the brothers is highly reminiscent of that of Abraham and Lot in Genesis 13:6 ff.

Chapter Five

1. The same exact verbs are used in both narratives: *va-yarotz likrato,* he ran towards him, *va-yehabbek,* he embraced [him], and *va-yenashek,* he kissed [him].
2. The parallelism is emphasized by the notion that Rachel, the youngest, was intended for Jacob (perhaps even betrothed to him), while Leah was meant for Esau. Midrash Sekhel Tov to Genesis 29:16–17.
3. The biblical writer emphasizes the role she played: "Rachel came with her father's flock; for she was a shepherdess."
4. Jacob is described as "watering *(va-yashk)* the flock," followed by "then Jacob kissed *(va-yishak)* Rachel." The soundplay stresses that Jacob responded to both the shepherdess and to her sheep.
5. Speiser, *Genesis,* p. 225, notes to Genesis 29:17 explain this popular etymology.
6. For the rabbis, this shows the power of prayer, since Leah's words annul the decree.
7. In the mystical tradition, Rachel represents *alma d'itgalia*— the physical world, while Leah is considered a paradigm of *alma d'itkasia,* the recondite spiritual world.
8. Waskow, *Godwrestling,* p. 6.
9. Jacob would not have to wait an additional seven years to marry Rachel, as understood by many modern biblical scholars as well as the rabbis, e.g., Bereshit Rabbah 70:19.
10. The text literally says that God saw that Leah was *"senuah"* (hated), though it probably should be translated as "unloved" or "not favored."
11. The term for womb is *rehem,* from the Hebrew root *rhm,* meaning compassion.
12. Actually it is the name in Hebrew of her second son, Shimon, which has the word *on,* affliction, clearly as a part of it.
13. According to the rabbis, Leah was the first person ever to praise God. As such, she sets the pattern for all future generations. See Bereshit Rabbah 71:5.
14. See Robert Alter's poignant comments in this regard in

The Art of Biblical Narrative, pp. 186–87.

15. Thomas Mann highlights Rachel's agony and jealousy by recreating Rachel's words in this manner. See his *Joseph and His Brothers,* trans. H.T. Lowe-Porter (Alfred A. Knopf: New York, l944), p. 219.

16. According to Ancient Near Eastern law, the handmaid is considered an extension of her mistress and the child is legally her mistress' child.

17. Both Rachel and Sarah utter the same words—*"Ibaneh mimenah,"* I will be built up through her. This also involves a wordplay on *"ben"* (son).

18. Note that Leah later gives birth to a daughter named Dinah (Genesis 30:21). The two sisters have children with similar names, again indicating their closeness.

19. The struggle with self is indicated by the use of the passive form of the verb *niphtalti* (I struggled) in this story.

20. Note that in Genesis 30:1, 9 the same verb (*va-taireh,* she saw) is used to describe both of them. Each was only able to see herself in relation to her sister's ability to bear children.

21. See Theodore Gaster, *Myth, Legend, Custom in the Old Testament* (New York: Harper and Row, l969), p. 200. The Hebrew root of *dudaim* is connected to the word for love.

22. Note that later Reuben would be the son who would sleep with Bilhah, *Rachel's* handmaid (Genesis 35:21). It is as if Reuben had a very intimate relationship with both sisters.

23. The phrases are identical in the two scenes. *Va-tetzei* is the same term used to describe her daughter Dinah's aggressive behavior in Genesis 34:1.

24. His name stands in contrast to the name Levi, meaning "to accompany" in Genesis 29:34. She names him Zebulun for *"yizbeleini ishi,"* my husband will be mine in perpetuity.

25. Dinah is the only one of Jacob's children whose name is not explained. There was no need to explain her name since Rachel already named one of her son's Dan, which is from the same root, and explained his name.

26. Fokkelman, *Narrative Art,* p. 140.

27. The name Joseph (Yosef) is a play both on the word *asaf,* here meaning "remove" or "gather up," and *yosef,* meaning "may he add."

28. The rabbis also stress that the birthright in effect was removed from Reuben and given to Joseph. B.T. *Baba Batra* 123a and

Yalqut Shimoni I, 125.

29. In the genealogy in Genesis 46, Leah is listed merely by name (v. 15), while Rachel is described as being "Jacob's wife" (v. 19).

Chapter Six

1. This is the second explanation of the name *Yosef*— "God will add," from the root *ysf.*
2. See Mann's *Joseph and His Brothers*, p. 352.
3. See also Wiesel, *Messengers*, p. 153.
4. The syntax of Genesis 37:2 is very odd and could be read as, "Joseph tended (guided, led) his brothers with the sheep," rather than "Joseph tended the sheep with his brothers."
5. Wiesel, *Messengers*, p. 156f.
6. Mann, *Joseph and His Brothers*, p. 320f.
7. The text in Genesis 37:4 pointedly emphasizes that the brothers hated Joseph by repeated usage of third person singular object, *him* in the sentence.
8. Wiesel, *Messengers,* p. 153.
9. The text emphasizes that Joseph responded because it was Jacob who asked, when it states, *"va-yomer lo hineinu,"* and Joseph responded to *him:* "Here I am."
10. Genesis 37:15 states, "A man came upon him wandering in the fields," *ve-hinei to'eh ba-sadeh.* The phrase "wandering in the fields" could refer to Joseph and not the stranger.
11. As in the story of Jacob's encounter, several midrashim assert that Joseph met an angel on the road. E.g., Bereshit Rabbah 84:14 and Pirkei d'Rabbi Eliezer, Chapter 38.
12. The words *"mah tevakesh,"* which are usually translated as "What are you looking for?" could mean, "What do you want, need?"
13. The syntactical emphasis of *"et ahai anochi mevakesh,* "it is *my brothers* for whom I am looking," also helps us understand what was going through Joseph's mind.
14. Genesis 37:17 reads: *"Nasu mi-zeh,"* [the brothers] moved from *this,* and it is not altogether clear what *zeh* (this) refers to—it could mean, "this one," i.e., Joseph.
15. Tamar remained in a state of *zikkah*, tied to Shelah. She could never remarry. As for Jacob, he refused to be comforted after Joseph's apparent death.
16. The symbolism of sheepshearing here is quite powerful. It hints at the uncovering that will occur in the encounter

between Judah and Tamar.

17. *Petah Einayim* (the Entrance to Einayim) literally means "the opening of the eyes."

18. Several midrashim emphasize that Judah's moral ascent began at Timnah with his confrontation with Tamar, e.g., Bereshit Rabbah 85:6.

19. The key word is "she saw." What Joseph and his brothers are able to perceive is crucial to the development of their relationship and their own growth.

20. This reminds us of Genesis 37:31 when the brothers dipped Joseph's coat in the blood of a kid in order to fool their father.

21. Steinmetz, *From Father to Son*, pp. 46 and 119–120. See Genesis 38:18, 27.

22. As Judah stares at the objects, the text says: *"Va-yaker Yehudah,"* Judah recognized—not only the seal, cord and staff, but himself and what he had done.

23. The crimson thread also alludes to the birthing of Jacob and Esau, as Esau is described as being of a red complexion.

24. Linguistically this runs parallel to 38:1 where "Judah went down from his brothers." The same verb *yarad* is used in both texts.

25. Samuel, *Certain People of the Book*, p. 330.

26. The play on the verb *nakar* is also a pun on *va-yitnaklu* in Genesis 37:18 when the brothers conspired against him. See Targum Onkelos to Genesis 42:7.

27. See Alter, *The Art of Biblical Narrative*, p. 164.

28. There are midrashim on Genesis 37 which speak of Joseph being in the pit for three days.

29. The same Hebrew root *arev* (pledge) is used here as it is in the Judah-Tamar story in Genesis 38:18.

30. The brothers carried with them many of the same spices which had been part of the Ishmaelite caravan when Joseph was sold to them (Genesis 37:25).

31. See Alter, *The Art of Biblical Narrative*, p. 143.

32. The term *na'ar* (boy) here used to refer to Benjamin, calls to mind his responsibility to Joseph as well, since Joseph was also referred to as a *na'ar*.

33. See Wiesel, *Messengers of God*, p. 161f. in this regard.

34. Joseph's words directed to Jacob were in the singular, as if he was talking to each one of them, and to the family as a whole.

35. Steinmetz, *From Father to Son*, p. 127.

36. Placing the boys on his knees was the formal procedure in the

Ancient Near East for adoption.

37. In Genesis 33:4 the same verbs are used—*nashak* (kiss) and *habak* (embrace).

38. The verb for crossing his hands is *sikel*, which can mean both to "act wisely" and "act foolishly." See, for example, Bereshit Rabbah, Chap. 97.

39. There are times when Manassah is listed before Ephraim, e.g., Numbers 26:28 and 34:23, which only serve to emphasize that they are considered equals. See also Waskow, *Godwrestling*, p. 19.

40. Jacob's opening word to them, *He-assefu* (gather together) was his way of emphasizing the need for unity among them. See Bereshit Rabbah 98:2 as well as Samuels, *Certain People of the Book*, p. 301.

41. The tradition that the messiah (ben David) will come from the tribe of Judah is based on Genesis 49:10 and the phrase *"ad ki yavo Shiloh."*

42. The phrase "Am I a substitute for God" echoes Jacob's statement in Genesis 30:2, but with no anger or animosity. It is a statement of his humility.

Epilogue

1. The positive attitude towards the Ephraimites probably originated following the aborted Bar Kochba revolt. See Joseph Heinemann, *Aggadot ve-Toldoteihen* (Jerusalem: Keter Publishing, 1974), pp. 133ff.

2. See Louis Ginzberg, *The Legends of the Jews* (Philadelphia: The Jewish Publication Society of America, 1968), v.1, p. 2, n. 10, and Heinemann, *Aggadot*, p. 131ff.

3. See Ephraim Urbach, *The Sages: Their Concepts and Beliefs*, trans. Israel Abrahams (Jerusalem: Magnes Press, 1975), v.1, p. 602.

4. There are many references to such a messianic figure scattered throughout Rabbinic Literature, especially in the apocalyptic midrashim.

5. This picture is a composite based on several eschatological midrashim. See Judah Ibn Shmuel's *Midrashei Ge'ulah* (Jerusalem: Mossad Bialik, 1954).

Ackerman, James S., Gros-Louis, Kenneth R.R. and Warshaw, Thayer S. eds. *Literary Interpretations of Biblical Narratives.* 2 Vols. Nashville: Abingdon Press, 1974, 1981.

Alter, Robert. *The Art of Biblical Narrative.* New York: Basic Books, 1981.

Banks, Lynne Reid. *Sarah and After: Five Women of the Old Testament.* New York: Doubleday, 1975.

Crites, Stephen. "The Narrative Quality of Experience," *The American Academy of Religion* 39 (1971): 291–311.

Fokkelman, J.P. *Narrative Art in Genesis.* Amsterdam: Van Gorcum, 1975.

Gellman, Marc. *Does God Have a Big Toe? Stories about Stories in the Bible.* New York: Harper and Row, 1989.

Iser, Wolfgang. *The Art of Reading: A Theory of the Aesthetic Response.* Baltimore: Johns Hopkins Press, 1979.

Jacobson, David C. *Modern Midrash: The Retelling of Traditional Jewish Narratives by Twentieth-Century Hebrew Writers.* Albany: State University of New York Press, 1987.

Kushner, Lawrence. *God Was in This Place & I, i Did Not Know.* Woodstock, Vt.: Jewish Lights Publishing, 1993.

Mann, Thomas. *Joseph and His Brothers.* Trans. H.T. Lowe-Porter. New York: Alfred A. Knopf, 1944.

Samuel, Maurice. *Certain People of the Book.* New York: Alfred A. Knopf, 1955.

Steinbeck, John. *East of Eden.* New York: Penguin Books, 1986.

Steinmetz, Devora. *From Father to Son: Kinship, Conflict and Continuity.* Louisville: John Knox Press, 1991.

Steinsaltz, Adin. *Biblical Images: Men and Women of the Bible.* New York: Basic Books, 1984.

Taking the First Fruit: Modern Women's Tales of the Bible. 2 Vols. published by the Women's Institute of Continuing Jewish Education, San Diego, 1981, 1989.

Waskow, Arthur. *Godwrestling.* New York: Schocken Books, 1978.

Wiesel, Elie. *Five Biblical Portraits.* South Bend: Notre Dame Press, 1981.

———. *Messengers of God: Biblical Portraits and Legends.* New York: Random House, 1976.

About Jewish Lights

People of all faiths and backgrounds yearn for books that attract, engage, educate, and spiritually inspire.

Our principal goal is to stimulate thought and help all people learn about who the Jewish People are, where they come from, and what the future can be made to hold. While people of our diverse Jewish heritage are the primary audience, our books speak to people in the Christian world as well and will broaden their understanding of Judaism and the roots of their own faith.

We bring to you authors who are at the forefront of spiritual thought and experience. While each has something different to say, they all say it in a voice that you can hear.

Our books are designed to welcome you and then to engage, stimulate, and inspire. We judge our success not only by whether or not our books are beautiful and commercially successful, but by whether or not they make a difference in your life.

For your information and convenience, at the back of this book we have provided a list of other Jewish Lights books you might find interesting and useful. They cover all the categories of your life:

Bar/Bat Mitzvah	Life Cycle
Bible Study / Midrash	Meditation
Children's Books	Parenting
Congregation Resources	Prayer
Current Events / History	Ritual / Sacred Practice
Ecology	Spirituality
Fiction: Mystery, Science Fiction	Theology / Philosophy
Grief / Healing	Travel
Holidays / Holy Days	Twelve Steps
Inspiration	Women's Interest
Kabbalah / Mysticism / Enneagram	

Dr. Norman J. Cohen is Provost of Hebrew Union College–Jewish Institute of Religion and Professor of Midrash. Widely recognized as one of the great rabbinic teachers of his generation, he frequently lectures to Jewish and Christian laypeople and scholars on the topic of *midrash*—finding contemporary meaning from the ancient biblical text—and has composed many of his own *midrashim*. He lives in the New York area with his wife Terry and their "blended family" of five children.

For People of All Faiths, All Backgrounds

JEWISH LIGHTS Publishing

www.jewishlights.com